THIRD EDITION

2

Skills for Success
READING AND WRITING

Joe McVeigh | Jennifer Bixby

OXFORD

UNIVERSITY PRESS

OXFORD
UNIVERSITY PRESS

198 Madison Avenue
New York, NY 10016 USA

Great Clarendon Street, Oxford, OX2 6DP, United Kingdom

Oxford University Press is a department of the University of Oxford.
It furthers the University's objective of excellence in research, scholarship,
and education by publishing worldwide. Oxford is a registered trade
mark of Oxford University Press in the UK and in certain other countries

ISBN: 978 0 19 490393 6   Student Book 2 with iQ Online pack
ISBN: 978 0 19 490369 1   Student Book 2 as pack component
ISBN: 978 0 19 490429 2   iQ Online student website

Printed in China

This book is printed on paper from certified and well-managed sources

ACKNOWLEDGMENTS

Back cover photograph: Oxford University Press building/David Fisher

*The Publishers would like to thank the following for their kind permission to reproduce
photographs and other copyright material*: 123RF: pp.87 (driver using GPS/
dolgachov), 125 (student reading/Dean Drobot), 135 (brain/nerthuz);
Alamy: pp.2 (taking photos/dpa picture alliance), 15 (line of people for
Starbucks/Kumar Sriskandan), 39 (choosing colours/ronstik), 49 ("The
Gates" public art installation by artists Christo and Jean-Claude/LEE
SNIDER), 53 (shaking hands/Westend61 GmbH), 63 (people using mobile
phones/David Gee 4), 73 (parked cars/SFL Travel), 74 (VR headset/ITAR-TASS
News Agency), 77 (medical student on phone/Aleksey Popov), 78 (medical
student VR/RioPatuca), 108 (going out of business/Kevin Foy), 149 (dog
walking/Hideo Kurihara), 151 (people doing Tai Chi in park/Michael
Brooks), 153 (Cheonggye Creek/Roman Babakin), 154 (girl and fox/AGAMI
Photo Agency), 157 (Al-Azhar Park/Claudia Wiens), 166 (purple trees/
DiscoverBA), 181 (mosquito netting/Mile 91/Ben Langdon), 184 (sneezing/
Everett Collection Historical); Blendtec: p.6 (Tom Dickson/Blendtec);
Getty: Cover (Andrius Gailiunas/EyeEm), pp.11 (people looking up/Hero
Images), 12 (looking at phone/Nick David), 25 (merchandise store/SOPA
Images), 26 (happy woman yellow/Flashpop), 30 (green/Eva-Katalin),
30 (red/Adam Blasberg), 31 (Queen in blue/Anwar Hussein), 31 (Queen
in green/Pool)Max Mumby), 31 (Queen in pink/Max Mumby/Indigo),
31 (Queen in red/Tim Graham), 36 (BP station/RONALDO SCHEMIDT/
Staff), 41 (jogging/Yagi Studio), 50 (dropping bottle/Chev Wilkinson),
54 (middle eastern men greeting/Katarina Premfors), 60 (suitcases/
monticelllo), 71 (student writing/PeopleImages), 84 (swimmer/AFP),
97 (VR lesson/VCG), 98 (bakery/Claudiad), 102 (Melted Iron Fireworks Show/
Lintao Zhang/Staff), 103 (welding in a dockyard/K M Asad), 110 (workers
in Lindt chocolate factory/Bloormberg), 121 (family business/Oliver
Rossi), 122 (reading/EmirMemedovski), 126 (student marking book/
DaniloAndjus), 133 (student helping/PeopleImages), 138 (Guiness World
record event/KRIT PHROMSAKLA NA SAKOLNAKORN), 145 (scientist/
Monty Rakusen), 146 (pedestrian walkway/fanjianhua), 150 (city park/
Eric Nathan), 156 (Singapore Gardens/Matteo Colombo), 160 (allotments/
SolStock), 162 (woman walking in spring park/David Soanes Photography),
170 (boy in mask/Clover No.7 Photography), 173 (college students/
skynesher), 185 (Medecins Sans Frontieres worker an patient/Spencer Platt),
193 (sneezing into elbow/AnthonyRosenberg), 195 (medical research/
William Taufic); Dr Jean Andersson-Swayze: p.180 (Dr. Jean Andersson-
Swayze); Oxford University Press: pp.29 (tree in blossom/Shutterstock),
142 (typing/Shutterstock; imtmphoto), 164 (Central park/Shutterstock;
Manamana); Shutterstock: pp.5 (Felix Baumgartner/Red Bull)Shutterstock),
13 (social media/Lepusinensis), 30 (blue/Yuri Shevtsov), 36 (UPS delivery
person/elbud), 54 (opening gift/Marko Poplasen), 83 (tennis racket and
balls/Natalya Yudina), 93 (baseball/JoeSAPhotos), 107 (Wall Street journal/
dennizn), 132 (student remembering/Motortion Films), 133 (student taking
notes/Monkey Business Images), 133 (Turkish man running/FotoAndalucia),
137 (rowing/John Kropewnicki), 169 (deer and tourist/Benny Marty),
176 (cold remedies/Syda Productions).

*Although every effort has been made to trace and contact copyright holders before
publication, this has not been possible in some cases. We apologize for any apparent
infringement of copyright and if notified, the publisher will be pleased to rectify any
errors or omissions at the earliest opportunity.*

Sources: p.36 'What Color is Business?' by Orwig Marketing Strategies, 2004.

ACKNOWLEDGMENTS

We would like to acknowledge the teachers from all over the world who participated in the development process and review of *Q: Skills for Success* Third Edition.

USA

Kate Austin, Avila University, MO; Sydney Bassett, Auburn Global University, AL; Michael Beamer, USC, CA; Renae Betten, CBU, CA; Pepper Boyer, Auburn Global University, AL; Marina Broeder, Mission College, CA; Thomas Brynmore, Auburn Global University, AL; Britta Burton, Mission College, CA; Kathleen Castello, Mission College, CA; Teresa Cheung, North Shore Communtiy College, MA; Shantall Colebrooke, Auburn Global University, AL; Kyle Cooper, Troy University, AL; Elizabeth Cox, Auburn Global University, AL; Ashley Ekers, Auburn Global University, AL; Rhonda Farley, Los Rios Community College, CA; Marcus Frame, Troy University, AL; Lora Glaser, Mission College, CA; Hala Hamka, Henry Ford College, MI; Shelley A. Harrington, Henry Ford College, MI; Barrett J. Heusch, Troy University, AL; Beth Hill, St. Charles Community College, MO; Patty Jones, Troy University, AL; Tom Justice, North Shore Community College, MA; Robert Klein, Troy University, AL; Wheeler Loreley, North Shore Communtiy College, MA; Patrick Maestas, Auburn Global University, AL; Elizabeth Merchant, Auburn Global University, AL; Rosemary Miketa, Henry Ford College, MI; Myo Myint, Mission College, CA; Lance Noe, Troy University, AL; Irene Pannatier, Auburn Global University, AL; Annie Percy, Troy University, AL; Erin Robinson, Troy University, AL; Juliane Rosner, Mission College, CA; Mary Stevens, North Shore Communtiy College, MA; Pamela Stewart, Henry Ford College, MI; Karen Tucker, Georgia Tech, GA; Amanda Wilcox, Auburn Global University, AL; Heike Williams, Auburn Global University, AL

Canada

Angelika Brunel, Collège Ahuntsic, QC; David Butler, English Language Institute, BC; Paul Edwards, Kwantlen Polytechnic University, BC; Cody Hawver, University of British Columbia, BC; Olivera Jovovic, Kwantlen Polytechnic University, BC; Tami Moffatt, Univeristy of British Columbia, BC; Dana Pynn, Vancouver Island University, BC

Latin America

Georgette Barreda, SENATI, Peru; Claudia Cecilia Díaz Romero, Colegio América, Mexico; Jeferson Ferro, Uninter, Brazil; Mayda Hernández, English Center, Mexico; Jose Ixtaccihuastl, Tecnologico de Tecomatlan, Mexico; Andreas Paulus Pabst, CBA Idiomas, Brazil; Amanda Carla Pas, Instituição de Ensino Santa Izildinha, Brazil; Allen Quesada Pacheco, University of Costa Rica, Costa Rica; Rolando Sánchez, Escuela Normal de Tecámac, Mexico; Luis Vasquez, CESNO, Mexico

Asia

Asami Atsuko, Women's University, Japan; Rene Bouchard, Chinzei Keiai Gakuenj, Japan; Francis Brannen, Sangmyoung University, South Korea; Haeyun Cho, Songang University, South Korea; Daniel Craig, Sangmyoung University, South Korea; Thomas Cuming, Royal Melbourne Institute of Technology, Vietnam; Jissen Joshi Daigaku, Women's University, Japan; Nguyen Duc Dat, OISP, Vietnam; Wayne Devitte, Tokai University, Japan; James D. Dunn, Tokai University, Japan; Fergus Hann, Tokai University, Japan; Michael Hood, Nihon University College of Commerce, Japan; Hideyuki Kashimoto, Shijonawate High School, Japan; David Kennedy, Nihon University, Japan; Anna Youngna Kim, Songang University, South Korea; Jae Phil Kim, Songang University, South Korea; Jaganathan Krishnasamy, GB Academy, Malaysia; Peter Laver, Incheon National University, South Korea; Hung Hoang Le, Ho Chi Minh City University of Technology, Vietnam; Hyon Sook Lee, Songang University, South Korea; Ji-seon Lee, Iruda English Institute, South Korea; Joo Young Lee, Songang University, South Korea; Phung Tu Luc, Ho Chi Minh City University of Technology, Vietnam; Richard Mansbridge, Hoa Sen University, Vietnam; Kahoko Matsumoto, Tokai University, Japan; Elizabeth May, Sangmyoung University, South Korea; Naoyuki Naganuma, Tokai University, Japan; Hiroko Nishikage, Taisho University, Japan; Yongjun Park, Sangji University, South Korea; Paul Rogers, Dongguk University, South Korea; Scott Schafer, Inha University, South Korea; Michael Schvaudner, Tokai University, Japan; Brendan Smith, RMIT University, School of Languages and English, Vietnam; Peter Snashall, Huachiew Chalermprakiat University, Thailand; Makoto Takeda, Sendai Third Senior High School, Japan; Peter Talley, Mahidol University, Faculty of ICT, Thailand; Byron Thigpen, Songang University, South Korea; Junko Yamaai, Tokai University, Japan; Junji Yamada, Taisho University, Japan; Sayoko Yamashita, Women's University, Japan; Masami Yukimori, Taisho University, Japan

Middle East and North Africa

Sajjad Ahmad, Taibah University, Saudi Arabia; Basma Alansari, Taibah University, Saudi Arabia; Marwa Al-ashqar, Taibah University, Saudi Arabia; Dr. Rashid Al-Khawaldeh, Taibah University, Saudi Arabia; Mohamed Almohamed, Taibah University, Saudi Arabia; Dr Musaad Alrahaili, Taibah University, Saudi Arabia; Hala Al Sammar, Kuwait University, Kuwait; Ahmed Alshammari, Taibah University, Saudi Arabia; Ahmed Alshamy, Taibah University, Saudi Arabia; Doniazad sultan AlShraideh, Taibah University, Saudi Arabia; Sahar Amer, Taibah University, Saudi Arabia; Nabeela Azam, Taibah University, Saudi Arabia; Hassan Bashir, Edex, Saudi Arabia; Rachel Batchilder, College of the North Atlantic, Qatar; Nicole Cuddie, Community College of Qatar, Qatar; Mahdi Duris, King Saud University, Saudi Arabia; Ahmed Ege, Institute of Public Administration, Saudi Arabia; Magda Fadle, Victoria College, Egypt; Mohammed Hassan, Taibah University, Saudi Arabia; Tom Hodgson, Community College of Qatar, Qatar; Ayub Agbar Khan, Taibah University, Saudi Arabia; Cynthia Le Joncour, Taibah University, Saudi Arabia; Ruari Alexander MacLeod, Community College of Qatar, Qatar; Nasir Mahmood, Taibah University, Saudi Arabia; Duria Salih Mahmoud, Taibah University, Saudi Arabia; Ameera McKoy, Taibah University, Saudi Arabia; Chaker Mhamdi, Buraimi University College, Oman; Baraa Shiekh Mohamed, Community College of Qatar, Qatar; Abduleelah Mohammed, Taibah University, Saudi Arabia; Shumaila Nasir, Taibah University, Saudi Arabia; Kevin Onwordi, Taibah University, Saudi Arabia; Dr. Navid Rahmani, Community College of Qatar, Qatar; Dr. Sabah Salman Sabbah, Community College of Qatar, Qatar; Salih, Taibah University, Saudi Arabia; Verna Santos-Nafrada, King Saud University, Saudi Arabia; Gamal Abdelfattah Shehata, Taibah University, Saudi Arabia; Ron Stefan, Institute of Public Administration, Saudi Arabia; Dr. Saad Torki, Imam Abdulrahman Bin Faisal University, Dammam, Saudi Arabia; Silvia Yafai, Applied Technology High School/Secondary Technical School, UAE; Mahmood Zar, Taibah University, Saudi Arabia; Thouraya Zheni, Taibah University, Saudi Arabia

Turkey

Sema Babacan, Istanbul Medipol University; Bilge Çöllüoğlu Yakar, Bilkent University; Liana Corniel, Koc University; Savas Geylanioglu, Izmir Bahcesehir Science and Technology College; Öznur Güler, Giresun University; Selen Bilginer Halefoğlu, Maltepe University; Ahmet Konukoğlu, Hasan Kalyoncu University; Mehmet Salih Yoğun, Gaziantep Hasan Kalyoncu University; Fatih Yücel, Beykent University

Europe

Amina Al Hashamia, University of Exeter, UK; Irina Gerasimova, Saint-Petersburg Mining University, Russia; Jodi, Las Dominicas, Spain; Marina Khanykova, School 179, Russia; Oksana Postnikova, Lingua Practica, Russia; Nina Vasilchenko, Soho-Bridge Language School, Russia

CRITICAL THINKING

The unique critical thinking approach of the *Q: Skills for Success* series has been further enhanced in the Third Edition. New features help you analyze, synthesize, and develop your ideas.

Unit question

The thought-provoking unit questions engage you with the topic and provide a critical thinking framework for the unit.

UNIT QUESTION

How can technology improve performance?

A Discuss these questions with your classmates.

1. What technology do you use every day? How does it improve your school performance?

2. Look at the photo. What is the girl doing? Where is she and what kind of technology do you think she is using?

B Listen to *The Q Classroom* online. Then answer these questions.

1. What four examples of technology do the students give?

2. What technology would you like to use to improve performance?

Analysis

You can discuss your opinion of each reading text and analyze how it changes your perspective on the unit question.

it help you practice certain situations or follow steps in a process? Does it help you learn and identify things? Explain.

iQ PRACTICE Go online for additional reading and comprehension. *Practice > Unit 4 > Activity 4*

WRITE WHAT YOU THINK

A. DISCUSS Discuss the questions in a group. Think about the Unit Question, How can technology improve performance?

1. How could virtual reality help you in your learning? Give specific examples.

2. Would you like to use virtual reality to learn how to speak English? Why or why not?

B. CREATE Choose one of the questions from Activity A and write a response. Look back at your Quick Write on page 77 as you think about what you learned.

NEW! Critical Thinking Strategy with video

Each unit includes a Critical Thinking Strategy with activities to give you step-by-step guidance in critical analysis of texts. An accompanying instructional video (available on iQ Online) provides extra support and examples.

CRITICAL THINKING STRATEGY

Restating

A good way to see if you understand an idea is to **restate** it. When you restate something, you write or say the idea using different words. If you repeat something exactly, it isn't always clear that you understand it. To restate the idea, you need to show that you understand what it means. When you restate, be sure not to use exactly the same language.

Original Statement	Restatement (using different words)
Every year, large companies spend millions of dollars on advertising.	Each year big companies use a lot of money to tell people about their products and services.
All over the world, companies use color to establish their brand and to encourage people to buy their products.	In many places, businesses use color, so people will know who they are and buy the things they make.

iQ PRACTICE Go online to watch the Critical Thinking Video and check your comprehension. *Practice > Unit 2 > Activity 8*

E. RESTATE Restate these sentences. Use different words and language to express the same idea.

1. Research studies show that yellow makes you feel happier.

2. We think carefully about color when we choose our clothes.

3. People who like to wear orange are cheerful and enjoy change.

4. There are not many colors with universal meaning.

5. In today's world, brown may seem like a boring color choice for a company.

NEW! Bloom's Taxonomy

Pink activity headings integrate verbs from Bloom's Taxonomy to help you see how each activity develops critical thinking skills.

F. APPLY Complete each statement with a word from the box. Use the

THREE TYPES OF VIDEO

UNIT VIDEO

The unit videos include high-interest documentaries and reports on a wide variety of subjects, all linked to the unit topic and question. All videos are from authentic sources such as the BBC and CBS.

NEW! "Work with the Video" pages guide you in watching, understanding, and discussing the unit videos. The activities help you see the connection to the Unit Question and the other texts in the unit.

CRITICAL THINKING VIDEO

NEW! Narrated by the Q series authors, these short videos give you further instruction into the Critical Thinking Strategy of each unit using engaging images and graphics. You can use them to get a deeper understanding of the Critical Thinking Strategy.

SKILLS VIDEO

NEW! These instructional videos provide illustrated explanations of skills and grammar points in the Student Book. They can be viewed in class or assigned for a flipped classroom, for homework, or for review. One skill video is available for every unit.

Easily access all videos in the Resources section of iQ Online.

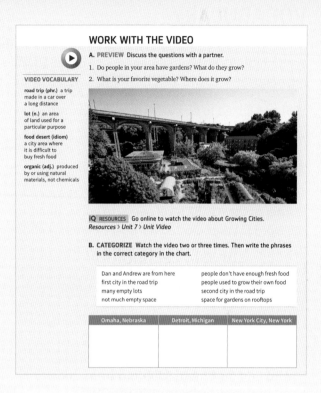

WORK WITH THE VIDEO

A. PREVIEW Discuss the questions with a partner.
1. Do people in your area have gardens? What do they grow?
2. What is your favorite vegetable? Where does it grow?

VIDEO VOCABULARY

road trip (phr.) a trip made in a car over a long distance

lot (n.) an area of land used for a particular purpose

food desert (idiom) a city area where it is difficult to buy fresh food

organic (adj.) produced by or using natural materials, not chemicals

iQ RESOURCES Go online to watch the video about Growing Cities. *Resources > Unit 7 > Unit Video*

B. CATEGORIZE Watch the video two or three times. Then write the phrases in the correct category in the chart.

Dan and Andrew are from here	people don't have enough fresh food
first city in the road trip	people used to grow their own food
many empty lots	second city in the road trip
not much empty space	space for gardens on rooftops

Omaha, Nebraska	Detroit, Michigan	New York City, New York

How to compare and contrast

Venn Diagram

Firefighter — Both — Police Officer

fights fires — *help people* — *fights crime*

stays at the station until called — *have dangerous jobs* — *works on the street*

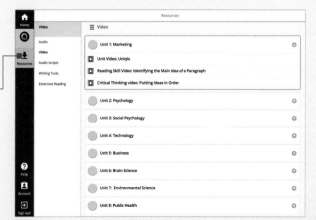

Resources		
Unit 1: Marketing		
Unit Video: Uniqlo		
Reading Skill Video: Identifying the Main Idea of a Paragraph		
Critical Thinking video: Putting Ideas in Order		
Unit 2: Psychology		
Unit 3: Social Psychology		
Unit 4: Technology		
Unit 5: Business		
Unit 6: Brain Science		
Unit 7: Environmental Science		
Unit 8: Public Health		

VOCABULARY

A research-based vocabulary program focuses on the words you need to know academically and professionally.

The vocabulary syllabus in *Q: Skills for Success* is correlated to the CEFR (see page 196) and linked to two word lists: the Oxford 3000 and the OPAL (Oxford Phrasal Academic Lexicon).

℔ OXFORD 3000

The Oxford 3000 lists the core words that every learner at the A1–B2 level needs to know. Items in the word list are selected for their frequency and usefulness from the Oxford English Corpus (a database of over 2 billion words).

Vocabulary Key
In vocabulary activities, ℔ shows you the word is in the Oxford 3000 and **OPAL** shows you the word or phrase is in the OPAL.

READING 1	**Unusual Ideas to Make a Buzz**
OBJECTIVE ▸	You are going to read an online article about how advertisers try to make things popular. Use the reading to gather information and ideas for your Unit Assignment.

PREVIEW THE READING

A. VOCABULARY Here are some words from Reading 1. Read their definitions. Then complete each sentence.

clear (*adjective*) ℔ OPAL easy to see, hear, or understand
connect (*verb*) ℔ OPAL to join or to link to something or someone
contribute (*verb*) ℔ OPAL to give or be a part of something with other people
express (*verb*) ℔ OPAL to say or show how you think or feel
find out (*verb phrase*) to get or discover information about something
spread (*verb*) ℔ to affect a large area or group of people
trend (*noun*) ℔ OPAL a general change or development

℔ Oxford 3000™ words   OPAL Oxford Phrasal Academic Lexicon

1. I don't know what time the mall opens. I'll go online to _find out_____.
2. Many Americans are buying smaller cars that use less gas. They are part of a _____ that started a few years ago.
3. A small fire can _____ quickly in a dry place.
4. Each member of the group should _____ equally to the project.
5. Thanks to the Internet, Jean can always _____ with her family, even though they live far away.
6. Because Doug and Liz don't speak Spanish well, they couldn't

---

OPAL
OXFORD PHRASAL ACADEMIC LEXICON

NEW! The OPAL is a collection of four word lists that provide an essential guide to the most important words and phrases to know for academic English. The word lists are based on the Oxford Corpus of Academic English and the British Academic Spoken English corpus. The OPAL includes both spoken and written academic English and both individual words and longer phrases.

Academic Language tips in the Student Book give information about how words and phrases from the OPAL are used and offer help with features such as collocations and phrasal verbs.

B. IDENTIFY Read the sentences. Write *N* (noun) or *V* (verb) for each bold word.

___V___ 1. My brothers **study** in the kitchen every night.
_____ 2. The **study** showed important changes in trends.
_____ 3. Steven wanted to **comment** on Lilly's presentation.
_____ 4. I saw the **comment** Penny wrote on the website.
_____ 5. My grandparents had an important **influence** on me.
_____ 6. My friends often **influence** my book choices.
_____ 7. Dr. Lee's **research** on weather is very interesting.
_____ 8. Tom will **research** many colleges before making a decision.
_____ 9. It is helpful to **review** your notes before a test.
_____10. After I read the movie **review**, I didn't want to see the movie.

ACADEMIC LANGUAGE
Some word forms are more common than others in academic writing. For example, *research* and *review* are more common as nouns than verbs.

_____ OPAL
Oxford Phrasal Academic Lexicon

C. APPLY Complete each sentence with a noun or a verb from Activity B. For verbs, use the correct form of the simple present.

1. Don _studies_____ in the library at night.
2. Faisal usually _____ books for the college newspaper.
3. The weather has a strong _____ on farmers' fruits and vegetables.
4. Ramona always _____ on my clothing.
5. Carol _____ news stories for her job at a magazine.
6. Allen's _____ is on the psychology of teenage shoppers.
7. There are only a few _____ from my teacher on my essay.
8. TV commercials often _____ our decisions about which products to buy.

iQ PRACTICE Go online for more practice with word families.
Practice ▸ Unit 1 ▸ Activity 9

EXTENSIVE READING

NEW! Extensive Reading is a program of reading for pleasure at a level that matches your language ability.

There are many benefits to Extensive Reading:

- It helps you to become a better reader in general.
- It helps to increase your reading speed.
- It can improve your reading comprehension.
- It increases your vocabulary range.
- It can improve your grammar and writing skills.
- It's great for motivation—reading something that is interesting for its own sake.

Each unit of *Q: Skills for Success Third Edition* has been aligned to an Oxford Graded Reader based on the appropriate topic and level of language proficiency. The first chapter of each recommended graded reader can be downloaded from iQ Online Resources.

UNIT 1

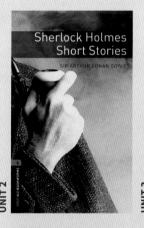

UNIT 2

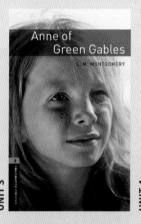

UNIT 3

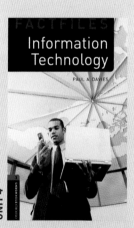

UNIT 4

UNIT 5

UNIT 6

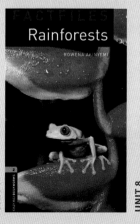

UNIT 7

UNIT 8

iQ ONLINE extends your learning beyond the classroom.

- Practice activities provide essential skills practice and support.
- Automatic grading and progress reports show you what you have mastered and where you need more practice.
- The Discussion Board allows you to discuss the Unit Questions and helps you develop your critical thinking.
- Essential resources such as audio and video are easy to access anytime.

NEW TO THE THIRD EDITION

- iQ Online is optimized for mobile use so you can use it on your phone.
- An updated interface allows easy navigation around the activities, tests, resources, and scores.
- New Critical Thinking Videos expand on the Critical Thinking Strategies in the Student Book.
- The Extensive Reading program helps you improve your vocabulary and reading skills.

How to use iQ ONLINE

Go to **Practice** to find additional practice and support to complement your learning in the classroom.

Go to **Resources** to find
- All Student Book video
- All Student Book audio
- Critical Thinking videos
- Skills videos
- Extensive Reading

Go to **Messages** and **Discussion Board** to communicate with your teacher and classmates.

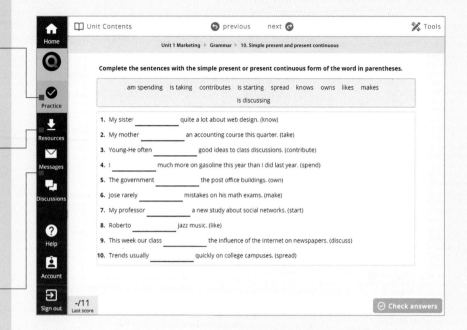

Progress bar shows you how many activities you have completed.

View your scores for all activities.

Online tests assigned by your teacher help you assess your progress and see where you still need more practice.

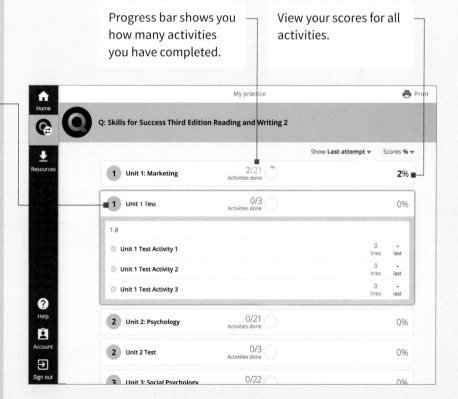

CONTENTS

Marketing

READING	identifying the main idea of a paragraph
CRITICAL THINKING	putting ideas in order
VOCABULARY	word families
WRITING	writing a descriptive paragraph
GRAMMAR	present continuous

Why does something become popular?

A. Discuss these questions with your classmates.

1. Do you and your friends like the same things? Do you wear the same clothes? Why do you think that is?

2. Look at the photo. Describe the people in the picture and what they are doing. What do you think makes a new product exciting?

B. Listen to *The Q Classroom* online. Then answer these questions.

1. Yuna thinks that popularity grows by word of mouth. Do you think that is true?

2. What is an example of another reason that something becomes popular?

iQ PRACTICE Go to the online discussion board to discuss the Unit Question with your classmates. *Practice > Unit 1 > Activity 1*

UNIT OBJECTIVE ▶ Read the articles. Gather information and ideas to write a descriptive paragraph about a current trend and why it is popular.

READING 1

Unusual Ideas to Make a Buzz

OBJECTIVE ▶

You are going to read an online article about how advertisers try to make things popular. Use the reading to gather information and ideas for your Unit Assignment.

PREVIEW THE READING

A. VOCABULARY Here are some words from Reading 1. Read their definitions. Then complete each sentence.

> **clear** (*adjective*) OPAL easy to see, hear, or understand
>
> **connect** (*verb*) OPAL to join or to link to something or someone
>
> **contribute** (*verb*) OPAL to give or be a part of something with other people
>
> **express** (*verb*) OPAL to say or show how you think or feel
>
> **find out** (*verb phrase*) to get or discover information about something
>
> **spread** (*verb*) to affect a large area or group of people
>
> **trend** (*noun*) OPAL a general change or development

 Oxford 3000™ words   **OPAL** Oxford Phrasal Academic Lexicon

1. I don't know what time the mall opens. I'll go online to _find out_.

2. Many Americans are buying smaller cars that use less gas. They are part of a _____ that started a few years ago.

3. A small fire can _____ quickly in a dry place.

4. Each member of the group should _____ equally to the project.

5. Thanks to the Internet, Jean can always _____ with her family, even though they live far away.

6. Because Doug and Liz don't speak Spanish well, they couldn't _____ themselves well when on vacation in Spain.

7. It was very _____ that Noriko didn't do her homework. She didn't know any answers during the class discussion.

iQ PRACTICE Go online for more practice with the vocabulary.
Practice > Unit 1 > Activities 2–3

B. PREVIEW Read the title and look at the pictures in the article about advertising. What do you think the article will say about advertising?

C. QUICK WRITE Why do you think that certain ideas or products become popular? Write three sentences. Include at least one example. Be sure to use this section for your Unit Assignment.

WORK WITH THE READING

A. INVESTIGATE Read the article and gather information about why something becomes popular.

UNUSUAL IDEAS TO MAKE A BUZZ

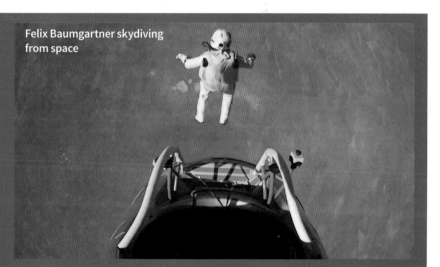
Felix Baumgartner skydiving from space

Introduction

1   Every year companies spend millions of dollars on advertising to create buzz about their products—in other words, to get people talking about them. Companies know that people like to talk about unusual, funny, and remarkable things. Nowadays, companies are using many creative ways to help products become more popular.

2   One idea that can **contribute** to popularity is to do something very unusual. Red Bull™ is a company that makes energy drinks. They want people to feel energetic when they think about Red Bull™. So they sponsored an unusual event: 43-year-old Felix Baumgartner jumped from 39 kilometers up in space to set a new world record for skydiving. He traveled more than 1,300 kilometers per hour in a spacesuit with Red Bull™'s name on it. This is part of a

controlling idea

new **trend** in advertising, in which companies pay for unusual events, hoping that customers will talk more about their products.

3   Some other companies choose to do something surprising so that people will remember their product and **spread** their idea. A good example is a company called Blendtec™. Tom Dickson, Blendtec™'s owner, had an idea to make his blenders look more interesting. He made videos showing his blenders mixing up unusual things. He put items like smartphones, rakes, or sports equipment into one of the machines and asked, "Will it blend?" People were surprised to see a blender cut a smartphone into small pieces. Everyone talked about the videos and wanted to **find out** more about the blenders. Dickson was invited to demonstrate his products

on TV shows. His blenders became much more popular, and he sold a lot more of them.

4   The company that makes Doritos™, a snack food, had a different idea about creating buzz. They decided to get their customers involved. So they began a competition. They asked customers to make their own TV ads. Then they

asked viewers to choose the ads that they liked the best. This created buzz because people like to participate and **express** their own opinions.

5   Another way to make a product popular is to **connect** it in people's minds with something that they see often. To improve sales, the maker of Kit Kat™ chocolate bars used advertisements that connected Kit Kat™ bars with coffee. They hoped that every time people drank coffee, they would think of Kit Kat™ bars. They were right. Sales improved by more than 50 percent when people connected Kit Kat™ bars with coffee.

6   There are many ways that advertisers hope to make their products become popular: doing something surprising or exciting, asking customers to get involved, or connecting the product with something that people see regularly. Whatever method is used, the result is **clear**: more buzz and more popularity.

B. IDENTIFY Match each product to the type of advertising used for it.

____ 1. Red Bull™   a. asked customers to make TV ads

____ 2. Blendtec™   b. connected the product with coffee

____ 3. Doritos™   c. used a skydiver

____ 4. Kit Kat™ bars   d. used their product to cut things to pieces

C. IDENTIFY Write the correct paragraph number next to each idea from the reading. Then underline the sentence where you found the answer.

____ a. People like to participate and express their own opinions.

____ b. Sometimes companies do surprising things to get people talking about a product.

____ c. Advertisers try to create buzz about their products.

____ d. Advertisers use different ways to make their products popular.

____ e. Some companies like to hold unusual events.

____ f. When people are surprised, they may talk about what they have seen.

D. EXPLAIN Answer the questions. Then circle the answer in the reading.

1. What does the word *buzz* mean?

   _____

2. How high was Felix Baumgartner when he jumped from space?

   _____

3. How fast did Felix Baumgartner travel on his skydiving adventure?

   _____

4. What items did Tom Dickson put in his blenders?

   _____

5. What method did Kit Kat™ use to get people to buy more candy?

   _____

6. By how much did Kit Kat™ sales improve?

   _____

7. Why do companies want to create buzz about their products?

   _____

E. EXPLAIN Complete each statement. Why did people talk about these products?

1. People talked about Red Bull™ because _____.

2. People talked about Blendtec™ because _____.

3. People thought about Doritos™ because _____.

4. People thought about Kit Kat™ because _____.

iQ PRACTICE Go online for additional reading and comprehension.
Practice > Unit 1 > Activity 4

WRITE WHAT YOU THINK

A. DISCUSS Discuss these questions in a group.

1. Which type of advertising from the reading do you think is most successful?

2. What is an advertisement that you can remember? Why do you remember it?

B. EXTEND Choose one question from Activity A and write a response. Look back at your Quick Write on page 5 as you think about what you learned.

Question: _____

My Response: _____

_____

_____

READING SKILL Identifying the main idea of a paragraph

TOPIC
||
Main

A **paragraph** is a group of sentences about one topic. The **main idea** of a paragraph is the most important point about the topic. You can often find the main idea in the first or second sentence of a paragraph. This is the **topic sentence**. The other sentences help explain or support the main idea. Identifying the main idea of a paragraph will help you to understand and remember what you read.

iQ RESOURCES Go online to watch the Reading Skill Video.
Resources > Video > Unit 1 > Reading Skill Video

A. IDENTIFY Read the paragraphs. Then circle the main ideas.

1. Experts often influence our actions and purchases. For example, a doctor on a TV health show may recommend a medication. Because the doctor is an expert in healthcare, we expect her to be very knowledgeable about what medicines are best. We are more likely to follow her advice.

2. Other consumers also influence our purchases. When a consumer uses a product, we listen to his or her opinion. On the Internet, consumers can write their opinions about products. For example, on some travel websites, people write reviews of hotels and restaurants. Online bookstores share reviews from ordinary people. These websites are very popular because they show that people are interested in consumers' opinions.

B. IDENTIFY Read the questions. Look back at Reading 1 on pages 5–6. Circle the correct answer for each question. Then write the key sentence from Reading 1 that helped you find the answer.

1. What is the main idea of paragraph 2?

    a. Felix Baumgartner set a new world record for skydiving from space.

    b. Drinking Red Bull™ may give you more energy.

    c. More companies are using unusual events to make people excited about their products.

    Key sentence: _____unusual , energy____

2. What is the main idea of paragraph 3?

   a. People will spread your idea if it is surprising.

   b. Blentec™'s blenders are very powerful; they can chop up anything.

   c. Tom Dickson had a good idea.

   Key sentence: _____ suprise , video , product _____

3. What is the main idea of paragraph 4?

   a. The company that makes Doritos™ started a competition.

   b. People could make their own TV ads.

   c. Doritos™ customers participated, so they felt more involved.

   Key sentence: _____ costomer , ads _____

4. What is the main idea of paragraph 5?

   a. The company used advertisement to connect Kit Kat™ bars with coffee.

   b. Connecting a product with something that people see often can help make it popular.

   c. The company hoped that sales would increase.

   Key sentence: _____ connect , coffe _____

iQ PRACTICE   Go online for more practice with identifying the main idea of a paragraph. *Practice ⟩ Unit 1 ⟩ Activity 5*

READING 2

How Do You Decide?

OBJECTIVE ▶

You are going to read an article from a business magazine about who influences our shopping choices. Use the article to gather information and ideas for your Unit Assignment.

PREVIEW THE READING

A. VOCABULARY Here are some words from Reading 2. Read the sentences. Circle the phrase that best matches the meaning of each underlined word.

1. Sometimes our friends can <u>influence</u> the decisions that we make.

   a. have an effect on

   b. postpone or delay

2. I love to talk with people and solve their problems. I would like to be a psychologist.

   a. a person who knows what other people are thinking

   b. a person who studies the human mind

3. When I got home from the mall, I showed my new purchase to my brother.

   a. a large box

   b. something that I bought

4. I highly recommend this book. It is a fascinating story.

   a. say that something is good

   b. say what something is about

5. The researcher looked at how often TV stations schedule children's programs.

   a. person who studies something

   b. person who manages something

6. The review of the new TV show was very good.

   a. an article that judges a show and tells if it is good

   b. an article that tells the story of a show

7. Alan is very popular and has an active social life.

   a. related to being in school and studying cultures

   b. related to meeting people and spending time with them

8. The scientists did an unusual study about the behavior of mice.

   a. college course

   b. research project

iQ PRACTICE Go online for more practice with the vocabulary.
Practice > Unit 1 > Activities 6–7

B. PREVIEW What do you think the article will say? Check (✓) your answer.

☐ People make their shopping choices because of what other people buy.

☐ People make their shopping choices because of what they like themselves.

C. QUICK WRITE Have you ever done something because all of your friends were doing it, too? What did you do? Did you enjoy it? Write your responses to the questions before you read the article. Be sure to use this section for your Unit Assignment.

WORK WITH THE READING

 A. INVESTIGATE Read the article and gather information about why something becomes popular.

HOW DO YOU **DECIDE?**

1   How do you decide what clothing or book to buy or which restaurant to eat at? You may think that you decide for yourself. But according to **studies** of human behavior, people around us greatly **influence** our choices and decisions.

2   **Psychologists** say that "**social** proof" influences us. Social proof is how other people's actions influence us. When we are not sure what to do, we look at what others are doing. The actions of other people are the "proof[1]" of the right thing to do. One example of this is a sidewalk experiment. If you stand still on a busy sidewalk and look up into the sky, no one will copy your actions. As one person, you probably won't influence other strangers. But social **researchers** discovered something interesting in New York City. When a group of four people looked up at the sky on a busy sidewalk, 80% of the passersby[2]

looked up at the sky. The passersby thought the four people must know something special. A group of people influences the behavior of others.

3   Businesses are very interested in understanding social proof. They want to influence us to buy their products. For that reason, social proof is very important in advertising. Four groups of people give social proof: experts[3], other consumers[4], crowds, and friends. First, experts often influence our actions and **purchases**. For example, an expert on a TV health show may **recommend** a medicine. Because the expert is knowledgeable, we may follow the advice. Advertisers use experts for social proof.

4   Other consumers also influence our purchases and show social proof. When a consumer uses a product, we listen to his or her opinion. On the Internet, consumers can express their opinions about products. For example, people write **reviews** of hotels and restaurants on travel websites. Online bookstores have book reviews from ordinary people. These websites are very popular because people are interested in consumers' opinions.

5   The third type of social proof comes from crowds. McDonald's, the fast food giant, has a sign on every restaurant, "Billions and Billions Served." The crowds of people who eat at McDonald's are the social proof of McDonald's popularity. In a recent experiment, a major hotel company wanted to decrease the number of towels it washed. The first hotel room sign said

---

[1] **proof:** facts that show something is true
[2] **passersby:** people who are walking by a place

[3] **experts:** people who know a lot about something
[4] **consumers:** people who buy things or use services

to say, "Most guests in this room reuse their towels. Will you?" 33% reused their towels. In this case, the actions of a group influenced other people. According to another study, when a restaurant marks certain dishes as "Our most popular," sales of those dishes increase by at least 13%. The behavior of other people can influence actions and purchases.

6   Finally, there is the social proof of friends. Friends influence us the most—more than experts, crowds, or other consumers. Our friends are usually more like us than other people, and we trust their recommendations. A quick text message or smartphone photo can show a new purchase. That is perhaps the best advertising of all, and for companies, it is free. It is simply friends talking about purchases. The next time you buy something, think about how you decided to buy it. It was probably a friend's influence!

"Help us help the environment. Please reuse your bath towel." Not many people did. The hotel changed the sign to say, "Most guests in this hotel reuse their towels. Will you?" Twenty-six percent of the guests then reused their towels. Finally, they changed the sign

B. IDENTIFY Circle the correct answer for each question.

1. What is the main idea of the reading?

    a. Different groups of people influence our purchases.

    b. Advertisers want to influence consumers.

    c. One example of social proof is experts talking about medicines on TV.

2. What is the main idea of paragraph 2?

    a. The sidewalk experiment shows that people are not influenced by an individual.

    b. The actions of other people will influence a person's behavior.

    c. Psychologists in New York City studied social proof.

C. EXPLAIN Answer the questions. Write the paragraph number where you found your answers.

1. What is social proof? Paragraph: _____

_____

2. Why are businesses interested in social proof? Paragraph: _____

_____

3. Why do people follow the advice of experts? Paragraph: _____

   _____

4. Why are travel and book-review websites popular? Paragraph: _____

   _____

5. What is probably the best advertising of all? Paragraph: _____

   _____

CRITICAL THINKING STRATEGY

Putting ideas in order

Reading passages can be organized in different ways. Sometimes the most important ideas come first. We say that those passages are organized in order of importance. Many reading passages in English are organized in a linear sequence. That is, the ideas flow from one to the other in a regular order. Sometimes the sentences state the order clearly using signal words like *first*, *second*, *next*, *then*, or *finally*. Sometimes the passage does not use those words. When you are trying to remember a reading passage, put the ideas in order as you read. Use the signal words to help you.

Look at the signal words in these sentences from Reading 2.

> **First**, experts often influence our actions and purchases.
> **Other** consumers **also** influence our purchases. . .
> The **third** type of social proof comes from crowds.
> **Finally**, there is the social proof of friends.

iQ PRACTICE   Go online to watch the Critical Thinking Video and check your comprehension. *Practice > Unit 1 > Activity 8*

D. **CATEGORIZE** According to the article, there are four groups of people who give social proof. Which groups do you think influence you the most? Number them from 1 (most important) to 4 (least important). Then explain why you gave the answer that you did.

_____ experts

_____ other consumers

_____ crowds

_____ friends

Your explanation: _____

_____

E. APPLY Complete the paragraph with words from the box.

advertising	consumers	friends	recommendations
behavior	experts	influence	

Social proof is how other people's actions _____ us. A group of
                                                          1

people can influence the _____ of others. _____
                                   2   3

can influence our actions and purchases because they are knowledgeable.

We also sometimes buy things because of other _____ ,
                                                       4

even if we don't know them. But the people who influence us most are our

_____ because we trust their _____ . That may be
         5   6

the best _____ of all.
                  7

F. IDENTIFY According to the magazine article, which of the following are examples of social proof? Check (✓) the boxes.

☐ 1. doing something because other people are doing it

☐ 2. buying something because of a magazine ad

☐ 3. staying at a hotel because of a review on a travel website

☐ 4. sharing a text message about a recent purchase

☐ 5. making a customer-produced video of a product

☐ 6. following the advice of an expert

☐ 7. watching a skydiver break a world record

G. DISCUSS Discuss the questions in a group. Look back at your Quick Write on page 10 as you think about what you learned.

1. Describe a time when you did something because of social proof.

2. Why do you think social proof is effective?

WORK WITH THE VIDEO

A. PREVIEW Are coffee shops popular where you live? Why do you think people go there: because they want to drink coffee or to sit and talk with friends?

VIDEO VOCABULARY

combine (v.) to join or mix two or more things together

service (n.) the work or the quality of work done by someone when serving a customer

chain (n.) a group of stores, hotels, etc. that are owned by the same person or company

atmosphere (n.) the mood or feeling of a place or situation

iQ RESOURCES Go online to watch the video about Starbucks coffee shops.
Resources › Video › Unit 1 › Unit Video

B. APPLY Watch the video two or three times. Choose the correct answers to complete the paragraph.

Starbucks was started by three ¹ *brothers / friends / business people*. The first store opened in Seattle in ² *1981 / 1971 / 1986*. Howard Schultz, a former ³ *chef / teacher / worker*, bought the company in 1987. Schultz had a great idea: combine ⁴ *Italian / Brazilian / American* café culture with Starbucks coffee and ⁵ *fast / cheap / friendly* service. It was an instant ⁶ *failure / success / business*, and the chain grew quickly between 1990 and 2010. But some people think that Starbucks is unfair to ⁷ *smaller / other / bigger* coffee shops. Howard Schultz agrees. The company's ⁸ *idea / brand / culture* is an important part of their success: people enjoy the ⁹ *temperature / atmosphere / price* as well as the ¹⁰ *coffee / cakes / conversation*.

C. DISCUSS Discuss the questions with a group.

1. There are many coffee shops. How did Starbucks make itself different than others?

2. Do you think a big company like Starbucks is unfair to small coffee shops? How?

3. Do you know of other small companies that became much bigger? Why do you think they were successful?

WRITE WHAT YOU THINK

SYNTHESIZE Think about Reading 1, Reading 2, and the unit video as you discuss these questions. Then choose one question and write a response.

1. In what ways do companies use social proof to encourage you to buy new products?

2. How do new trends begin? Give an example of a new trend. Why did it become popular?

VOCABULARY SKILL Word families

Learning about **word families** can help you improve your vocabulary. Word families are groups of words that come from the same root. If you know the meaning of the *noun form* of a word, you may also recognize the *verb form*.

In some word families, the noun form and the verb form are the same.

His teacher had a strong <u>influence</u> on him.   Parents <u>influence</u> their children.

noun   verb

TIP FOR SUCCESS
To help you determine if a word is a noun or a verb, remember that a noun is a person, place, or object, and a verb usually shows action.

A. IDENTIFY Look at the pairs of words. Decide if each word is a noun or a verb. Then write the words in the correct side of the chart. Use a dictionary to help you.

~~choice/choose~~
connect/connection
contribution/contribute

discuss/discussion
enjoy/enjoyment
gift/give

inform/information
thought/think

Nouns	Verbs
choice	choose

B. IDENTIFY Read the sentences. Write *N* (noun) or *V* (verb) for each bold word.

<u>V</u> 1. My brothers **study** in the kitchen every night.

___ 2. The **study** showed important changes in trends.

___ 3. Steven wanted to **comment** on Lilly's presentation.

___ 4. I saw the **comment** Penny wrote on the website.

___ 5. My grandparents had an important **influence** on me.

___ 6. My friends often **influence** my book choices.

___ 7. Dr. Lee's **research** on weather is very interesting.

___ 8. Tom will **research** many colleges before making a decision.

___ 9. It is helpful to **review** your notes before a test.

___ 10. After I read the movie **review**, I didn't want to see the movie.

ACADEMIC LANGUAGE

Some word forms are more common than others in academic writing. For example, *research* and *review* are more common as nouns than verbs.

___| OPAL
Oxford Phrasal Academic Lexicon

C. APPLY Complete each sentence with a noun or a verb from Activity B. For verbs, use the correct form of the simple present.

1. Don <u>studies</u> in the library at night.

2. Faisal usually _____ books for the college newspaper.

3. The weather has a strong _____ on farmers' fruits and vegetables.

4. Ramona always _____ on my clothing.

5. Carol _____ news stories for her job at a magazine.

6. Allen's _____ is on the psychology of teenage shoppers.

7. There are only a few _____ from my teacher on my essay.

8. TV commercials often _____ our decisions about which products to buy.

iQ PRACTICE Go online for more practice with word families.
Practice > Unit 1 > Activity 9

WRITING

OBJECTIVE ▶

At the end of this unit, you will write a paragraph that describes a trend and explains why it is popular. This paragraph will include specific information from the readings and your own ideas.

WRITING SKILL Writing a descriptive paragraph

When you write a **descriptive paragraph**, you give the reader information about your topic. The following are important elements in a descriptive paragraph.

- A *topic sentence* introduces what you are going to describe. The topic sentence introduces the *topic* or subject of the paragraph. It also gives the *controlling idea,* which is what you want to say about the topic.

topic   controlling idea

Exciting events are one way for companies to gain interest in their products.
Word of mouth is a useful and inexpensive way to advertise.

- In a descriptive paragraph, your **supporting sentences** help the reader understand the topic. They use descriptive words, such as adjectives and details, to create a clear picture of your topic.

Felix Baumgartner's jump from space was very **exciting**.

He traveled more than 1,300 kilometers per hour in a spacesuit with Red Bull™'s name on it.

The Blendtec™ video suddenly became **extremely popular** online.

People were surprised to see a blender **cut a smartphone into small pieces**.

- A **concluding sentence** summarizes your ideas.

Because many people saw the video of Baumgartner's jump, they connected Red Bull™ with excitement.

The company sold more blenders because people were talking about their product.

A. WRITING MODEL Read the model paragraph below. Label the circled parts of the paragraph. Write *TS* (topic sentence), *SS* (supporting sentence), or *CS* (concluding sentence).

_____   ⟨Psychologists say that "social proof" influences us.⟩ Social proof is how other people's actions influence us. When we are not sure what to do, we look at what others are doing. The actions of other people are the "proof" of the right thing to do. ⟨One example of this is a sidewalk experiment.⟩ If you stand still on a busy sidewalk and look up, no one will copy your actions. As one person, you probably won't influence others. But social researchers discovered something interesting in New York City. ⟨When a group of four people looked up at the sky on a busy sidewalk, 80% of the passersby looked up also.⟩ The passersby thought the four people must know something special. ⟨A group of people influences the behavior of others.⟩

B. IDENTIFY Match each part of the paragraph in Activity A with its purpose.

____ 1. topic sentence   a. summarizes your ideas

____ 2. supporting sentences   b. introduces what you will describe

____ 3. concluding sentence   c. help the reader understand the topic

C. IDENTIFY Circle the topic sentence in this paragraph from Reading 2.

Finally, there is the social proof of friends. Friends influence us the most— more than experts, crowds, or other consumers. Our friends are usually more like us than other people, and we trust their recommendations. A quick text message or smartphone photo can show a new purchase. That is perhaps the best advertising of all, and for companies, it is free. It is simply friends talking about purchases. The next time you buy something, think about how you decided to buy it. It was probably a friend's influence!

D. DISCUSS Circle the best topic sentence for each group of sentences. Discuss your answers with a classmate. What is the topic? What is the controlling idea?

1. a. For example, torn jeans were popular years ago, but not now.

   b. The most popular clothing is not always popular the next year.

   c. I buy new clothes every year to be fashionable.

2. a. The computer lab is open from 9:00 until 2:00.

   b. For example, Brett doesn't have a computer at home.

   c. Classroom computers are very helpful for students.

3. a. Many older adults need a lesson on how to use a smartphone.

   b. My grandfather can't send a text message on his smartphone.

   c. My grandmother keeps forgetting how to download apps.

E. EVALUATE Read the paragraphs. Then choose the best topic sentence.

1. People of all ages are affected by this trend. Some people think that every job will require people to use some kind of technology. Some people even think that soon there will be computers that people actually wear as part of their clothing. Others think that these ideas will never happen. But there is no question that more and more technology is a part of everyday life.

   a. It doesn't matter what your age is.

   b. Throughout the world, people are using more and more technology.

   c. Technology is getting smaller all the time.

2. Because of this, people from Africa to Australia are buying the same clothes, eating the same foods, and watching the same television shows. Some people are worried that people are losing parts of their history and culture and becoming more like people in other countries. In France, for example, there is a group that tries to be sure that there are enough TV shows that are made in France, not from other countries.

a. Most people like the same things.

b. Through the power of technology, people are becoming more similar all around the world.

c. People are the same all over the world.

F. **WRITING MODEL** Read a student's model paragraph. Then write a topic sentence for the paragraph. Compare your topic sentence with a partner's.

_____

_____.

First of all, I usually don't like the new fashion trends. I have my own style. I usually buy well-made clothes, and I wear them for many years. Some of my clothes are more than five years old. Buying new clothes every year is very expensive. For example, trendy jeans cost over $100. I buy clothes that I like, not the latest trends.

G. **CREATE** Work with a partner. Complete the graphic organizer below. Write a topic sentence about something that is popular. Make sure your sentence contains a controlling idea. Then write two supporting ideas in the boxes. Your supporting ideas will help to describe your topic.

Topic sentence

Supporting idea

Supporting idea

H. COMPOSE Take the ideas from Activity G and write a descriptive paragraph about the topic. Include a topic sentence, supporting sentences, and a concluding sentence.

I. EVALUATE Ask a classmate to read and comment on your writing. Use the peer-review checklist.

PEER-REVIEW CHECKLIST
☐ Does the paragraph have a topic sentence with a clear controlling idea?
☐ Do the ideas in the supporting sentences relate clearly to the topic?
☐ Do the supporting sentences use adjectives and details to help you understand the topic better?
☐ Does the paragraph have a clear conclusion?

iQ PRACTICE Go online for more practice with descriptive paragraphs. *Practice > Unit 1 > Activity 10*

GRAMMAR Present continuous

Use the **present continuous** to talk about activities in progress at the time of writing or that have started but not finished.

Ramon **is talking** on the phone. He**'s finding out** the arrival time. (activities in progress)

We **are learning** about how ideas spread. (action started but not finished)

The new trend **is contributing** to higher costs. (change in progress)

Use the present continuous with words like *today, this week,* or time periods around the present.

This week, I **am studying** for exams.

These days, more guests **are reusing** their towels in hotels.

To form the present continuous, use the verb *to be* and then the *–ing* form of the main verb.

If the verb ends in *e*, delete the *e* and add *–ing*.

use → using   change → changing   lose → losing

Use the present continuous to talk about changes. For example, *changing, becoming, growing, increasing.*

TV ads **are becoming** like short movies.

The Internet **is changing** the way companies advertise.

Some verbs are not used with the present continuous. For example, *know, want, need, understand, like, love, believe, see, hear.*

I **want** to go with you, but I'm studying right now.

A. IDENTIFY Read the paragraph and circle verbs in the present continuous. Then answer the questions. Compare your answers with a partner.

1. Nowadays more and more companies are making advertisements that involve their customers. These companies are using many creative ways to help products become more popular. Researchers believe social proof is the idea behind this trend. This is because when we are not sure what to do, we look at what others are doing. More and more people are using smartphones and social media to share news about their purchases with their friends.

2. Why is the present continuous used in the first sentence?

   Nowadays, more and more companies are making advertisements that involve their customers.

   a. The action happens all the time.

   b. The action is taking place at the time of writing.

   c. The action is completed.

3. Why is the present continuous **not** used in this sentence?

   Researchers believe social proof is the idea behind this trend.

   a. The action is happening now.

   b. The action is taking place at the time of writing.

   c. The verb *believe* is not used in the present continuous.

B. APPLY Complete each sentence with the present continuous of the word in parentheses. Remember to add the correct form of the verb *be*.

1. Companies _____ (use) new ways of advertising to reach their customers.

2. Young people _____ (follow) new trends in fashion.

3. Teenagers _____ (copy) their friends and doing the same things.

4. They _____ (buy) the same clothing and the same devices.

5. Customers _____ (complain) that the advertisements are too boring.

6. Through online videos, Blendtec™ _____ (spread) the word about its products.

7. The company _____ (improve) its reputation by using customers to share their ideas.

8. This month our store isn't advertising on the radio, so we _____ _____ (lose) some customers.

9. I think you _____ (be) very silly about following new trends.

iQ PRACTICE Go online for more practice with the present continuous.
Practice > Unit 1 > Activity 11

iQ PRACTICE Go online for the Grammar Expansion: simple present.
Practice > Unit 1 > Activity 12

UNIT ASSIGNMENT Write a descriptive paragraph

OBJECTIVE ▶

In this assignment, you will describe a trend that interests you and explain why this trend is popular. As you prepare your descriptive paragraph, think about the Unit Question, "Why does something become popular?" Use information from Reading 1, Reading 2, the unit video, and your work in this unit to support your paragraph. Refer to the Self-Assessment checklist on page 24.

iQ PRACTICE Go online to the Writing Tutor to read a model descriptive paragraph. *Practice > Unit 1 > Activity 13*

PLAN AND WRITE

TIP FOR SUCCESS

When you brainstorm ideas before writing, think of as many ideas as you can. You don't need to use all of them. Just use the best ones.

A. BRAINSTORM Think about current trends. Write down as many ideas as you can. For example, you can list trends in cars, food, or technology.

_____

_____

_____

B. PLAN Choose one trend from your list in Activity A as your topic. Answer the questions. Then tell your partner about your topic.

1. What is the trend? Describe it.

_____

_____

2. Does the trend help people connect with others? How?

_____

_____

3. Why is the trend popular? What is new and different about it?

_____

_____

4. How did this trend start and spread or become popular?

_____

_____

iQ RESOURCES Go online to download and complete the outline for your descriptive paragraph. *Resources > Writing Tools > Unit 1 > Outline*

C. WRITE Use your planning notes to write your descriptive paragraph.

1. Write a topic sentence for your paragraph. Include your topic and your controlling idea in your sentence. Then use some of your answers from Activity B to write your paragraph.

2. Look at the Self-Assessment checklist to guide your writing.

iQ PRACTICE Go online to the Writing Tutor to write your assignment. *Practice > Unit 1 > Activity 14*

REVISE AND EDIT

iQ RESOURCES Go online to download the peer review worksheet. *Resources > Writing Tools > Unit 1 > Peer Review Worksheet*

A. PEER REVIEW Read your partner's paragraph. Then use the Peer Review worksheet. Discuss the review with your partner.

B. REWRITE Based on your partner's review, revise and rewrite your paragraph.

WRITING TIP

Read your paragraph more than once. For example, read once for ideas and to be sure you support your topic sentence. Read again to check your verb tenses.

C. EDIT Complete the Self-Assessment checklist as you prepare to write the final draft of your paragraph. Be prepared to hand in your work or discuss it in class.

SELF-ASSESSMENT	Yes	No
Do all the sentences in the paragraph support your topic sentence?	☐	☐
Do you have a concluding sentence that summarizes your ideas?	☐	☐
Underline all the verbs in the present continuous. Are they correct?	☐	☐
Does your paragraph include vocabulary from the unit?	☐	☐

D. REFLECT Discuss these questions with a partner or group.

1. What is something new you learned in this unit?

2. Look back at the Unit Question—Why does something become popular? Is your answer different now than when you started the unit? If yes, how is it different? Why?

iQ PRACTICE Go to the online discussion board to discuss the questions. *Practice > Unit 1 > Activity 15*

TRACK YOUR SUCCESS

iQ PRACTICE Go online to check the words and phrases you have learned in this unit. *Practice ⟩ Unit 1 ⟩ Activity 16*

Check (✓) the skills you learned. If you need more work on a skill, refer to the page(s) in parentheses.

READING	☐ I can identify the main idea of a paragraph. (p. 8)
CRITICAL THINKING	☐ I can put ideas in order. (p. 13)
VOCABULARY	☐ I can use noun and verb forms in word families. (p. 16)
WRITING	☐ I can write a descriptive paragraph. (p. 18)
GRAMMAR	☐ I can use the present continuous. (p. 21)
OBJECTIVE ▶	☐ I can gather information and ideas to write a descriptive paragraph about a current trend and why it is popular.

2

Psychology

How do colors affect our behavior?

A. Discuss these questions with your classmates.

1. What's your favorite color? Why do you like it?

2. Imagine that you walk into a room that has yellow walls. How does that color make you feel?

3. Look at the photo. Describe how it makes you feel. Do you think you would have a different reaction if the clothes and walls were a different color?

B. Listen to *The Q Classroom* online. Then answer these questions.

1. What colors did the students mention? How do the colors make the students behave differently?

2. What color would you like to paint your room? Why?

iQ PRACTICE Go to the online discussion board to discuss the Unit Question with your classmates. *Practice > Unit 2 > Activity 1*

UNIT OBJECTIVE

Read the articles. Gather information and ideas to write a proposal about the colors you will use for a new business.

READING 1

What Colors Do You Like to Wear?

OBJECTIVE ▶

You are going to read an article about colors and what they tell us about the people who wear them. Use the article to gather information and ideas for your Unit Assignment.

PREVIEW THE READING

A. VOCABULARY Here are some words from Reading 1. Read the sentences. Then write each underlined word next to the correct definition.

1. The weather can affect us. When it's cold and rainy, many people feel sad.

2. Although Armando is Jake's brother, his character is completely different.

3. When Khalid came to Miami from Saudi Arabia, it was hard for him to understand some things about American culture. For example, he didn't understand why people wore jeans to nice restaurants.

4. Ana is interested in the way that people think and act. She wants to study psychology.

5. The color red has many meanings. It can represent danger, anger, or action.

6. Tom is unaware of how loudly he talks on his cell phone, so he keeps doing it.

7. It's a universal belief that friendship is important. I don't know anyone who doesn't think so.

8. I like our language school. There are a variety of fun activities.

a. _____ (verb) to be a picture, example, or sign of something

b. _____ (verb) to make someone or something change in a particular way; to influence someone or something

c. _____ (noun) a number of different kinds of things

d. _____ (noun) the ideas, beliefs, and ways of doing things in a particular society or country

e. _____ (adjective) involving everyone in the world or in a certain group

f. _____ (adjective) not knowing or noticing someone or something

g. _____ (*noun*) the study of the mind and the way that people behave

h. _____ (*noun*) the qualities that make someone or something different from other people or things

iQ PRACTICE   Go online for more practice with the vocabulary.
Practice > Unit 2 > Activities 2–3

B. PREVIEW Look at the title of the article, the photos, and the captions. Answer these questions.

1. What do you think the text will be about?

   _____

2. How many photos do you see? What do the captions describe?

   _____

3. What does the color green make Elizabeth Sweetheart think about?

   _____

4. Look at the last paragraph. What is the final conclusion of the text?

   _____

C. QUICK WRITE Think about the color red. Write a few sentences about how it makes you feel. If possible, give examples to support your answers. Be sure to use this section for your Unit Assignment.

WORK WITH THE READING

 A. INVESTIGATE Read the textbook article and gather information about how colors affect the way we behave.

What Colors Do You Like to Wear?

1   Do you like some colors more than others? Most people do. We think carefully about color when we choose our clothes or a new backpack. But you may be **unaware** that the colors that you choose can tell us something about you. If you look carefully, you will find that even if you have clothes in a **variety** of different colors, there is always one color that you like more. This color probably makes you feel more comfortable. That is the color that can tell us something about your **character**.

ACADEMIC LANGUAGE
The word *field* can mean "an area of study or knowledge." The phrase *in the field of* is common in academic writing. You can also use *in the area of* to mean the same thing.

⎯⎯⎯⎯⎯ OPAL
Oxford Phrasal Academic Lexicon

2   For example, maybe you like to wear black. According to research in the field of **psychology**, the color black suggests that you are serious and intelligent. Maybe that is the reason that university students wear a long black robe when they graduate. Or you might choose to wear black as a sign of respect for someone who died. What if you like to wear blue? People who wear blue are confident and reliable. That may be why many uniforms and business suits are blue and it is a good color to wear to a job interview. Scientists at the University of British Columbia found that blue gives a feeling of calm and peacefulness. Psychologists say that people who wear blue are good and reliable parents and workers. And, of course, one of the most popular items of clothing is blue: blue jeans.

Tom Le's favorite color is red. He says, "I like red because it's a warm, bright color. Red makes me feel happy."

Valeria McCullock wears only blue. She says blue makes her feel peaceful. "Wearing blue for me is being in a dream all day," she says.

Elizabeth Sweetheart dresses in green. It makes her think of nature—trees, flowers, grass. "I missed nature when I moved to New York," she says.

3   Yellow is the color of happiness, sun, and laughter. Research studies show that yellow makes you feel happier. Experts say that yellow clothing is often used by active, creative people. People who wear bright shades of red get a lot of attention. They may have a lot of energy and get excited easily. Scientists from the University of Amsterdam say that the color green gives you a good mood. It **represents** peace and happiness. People who wear green may be very active and take good care of money. They are also caring and kind.

4   Orange is a fun color and also very warm. Those who like to wear orange are cheerful and enjoy change. The color white suggests something new. That's why many people decide to wear something white when they are starting something new in their life, like getting married. People who like to wear white are very neat and organized in everything they do.

5   Of course, colors may have different meanings in different **cultures**. A color may represent good feelings in one culture but bad feelings in another. For example, in the United States, white represents goodness. However, in India, China, and Japan, white can mean death! There are not many colors with **universal** meaning that are viewed exactly the same way in every country.

6   Colors can **affect** people in different ways. They can affect how you think, feel, and act. So be careful what colors you wear. Are you sending the right message?

Queen Elizabeth II of England is famous for her colorful outfits.

B. CATEGORIZE Read the statements. Write *T* (true) or *F* (false). Then correct each false statement to make it true. Write the paragraph number where the answer is found.

____ 1. We can learn something about you by what colors you choose to wear.

Paragraph: ____ _____

____ 2. People who wear black are fun-loving and silly.

Paragraph: ____ _____

____ 3. Yellow is the color of happiness and laughter.

Paragraph: ____ _____

____ 4. People who wear orange are not very happy.

Paragraph: ____ _____

____ 5. The color white has different meanings in different countries.

Paragraph: ____ _____

C. IDENTIFY Write what each color means according to the article. Give as many answers as possible.

blue	yellow	green	white
confident	laughter	peace	something new

D. COMPOSE Use the words to write sentences. Use information from the reading.

1. most people / think carefully

   Most people think carefully about color.

2. According to research / black / intelligent

   _____

3. Blue / feeling / calm

   _____

4. Yellow clothing / active / creative

   _____

5. Scientists / green / good mood

   _____

6. Colors / different meanings / cultures

   _____

E. COMPOSE For each paragraph of the article, complete one of the main ideas in your own words. Use some of the phrases from the box.

can tell us something	suggests that you
makes you feel	when they are starting something new
have different meanings	affect people in different ways

1. The colors you choose _can tell us something about you._

2. The color black _____

   _____

3. Yellow _____

_____

4. People wear white _____

_____

5. Colors may _____

_____

6. Colors can _____

_____

iQ PRACTICE Go online for additional reading and comprehension.
Practice › Unit 2 › Activity 4

WRITE WHAT YOU THINK

A. DISCUSS Discuss these questions in a group. Then choose one question and write a response.

1. According to the article, the colors you prefer can tell us something about your character. What do you think the colors you like have to say about you?

2. Think about the color of your bedroom or living room. How does the color make you feel? Would you like to change the color? Why or why not?

B. COMPOSE Choose one of the questions and write a response. Look back at your Quick Write on page 29 as you think about what you learned.

READING SKILL Getting meaning from context

If you find a word you don't know in a text, you can use the **context** to help you understand the meaning of the word. The context is the other words near the unknown word.

                                    context
It was a **joyful** celebration. Everyone was very happy.

                                            context
The red sign told me that there was **danger** and some possibility of injury.

From the context, you can understand that the word *joyful* means "very happy." From the example, you can understand that *danger* means "a chance that someone might get hurt."

A. APPLY Read these sentences. Circle the word or words that give the context for the bold word in each sentence.

1. Even if you have clothes in a **variety** of different colors, there is always one color that you like more.

2. It makes her think of **nature**—trees, flowers, grass.

3. University students wear a long, black **robe** when they graduate.

4. The **uniforms** worn by police officers are often blue.

5. People who wear blue are good and **reliable** parents and workers. Others can depend on them.

6. You can paint your room in a variety of **shades** of green from light to dark.

B. RESTATE Write a definition for each word from Activity A. Then check your definitions in your dictionary.

1. variety   _____

2. nature   _____

3. robe   _____

4. uniform   _____

5. reliable   _____

6. shade   _____

iQ PRACTICE   Go online for more practice with getting meaning from context. *Practice > Unit 1 > Activity 5*

READING 2

The Importance of Color in Business

OBJECTIVE ▶

You are going to read an article about how colors can affect the way people think about companies. Use the article to gather information and ideas for your Unit Assignment.

PREVIEW THE READING

VOCABULARY SKILL REVIEW

In Unit 1, you learned about words that are both nouns and verbs. Look at the vocabulary in this activity. Which two vocabulary words are both nouns and verbs?

A. VOCABULARY Here are some words from Reading 2. Read the sentences. Circle the answer that best matches the meaning of each underlined word.

1. <u>Advertising</u> on social media helped the restaurant increase its business.

   a. writing articles
   b. talking to customers
   c. telling people about products

2. Choosing a college is difficult. I have to carefully <u>consider</u> all my choices.

   a. think about
   b. be worried about
   c. measure

3. My car is not very <u>dependable</u>. My battery died three times this month!

   a. important
   b. forceful
   c. reliable

4. I'm going to <u>encourage</u> Jorge to apply for the new job at the radio station. I think it's the perfect job for him.

   a. convince
   b. research
   c. command

5. Our family recycles paper and plastic to help protect the <u>environment</u>.

   a. machines
   b. natural world
   c. people

6. She left her job because she wants to <u>establish</u> her own company.

   a. create
   b. sell
   c. research

7. We didn't <u>notice</u> him leave the classroom.

   a. tell that
   b. see and be aware of
   c. show or describe

8. A <u>service</u> that many hotels offer is helping with luggage.

   a. relationship between companies
   b. thing that a company does for you
   c. rule that a company follows

iQ PRACTICE Go online for more practice with the vocabulary.
Practice > Unit 2 > Activities 6–7

B. PREVIEW Preview the article and circle the names of six companies. Then discuss the companies with a partner. What do you know about these companies? What are their products or services?

C. QUICK WRITE How do colors help people remember a company and its name? How do colors affect customers? Write a few sentences about the topic. Be sure to use this section for your Unit Assignment.

WORK WITH THE READING

The Importance of Color in Business

A BP gas station

1   If you walk into a McDonald's restaurant, what colors will you see? Probably yellow and red. And when you think about McDonald's, you will think about those two bright and cheerful colors. Every year large companies spend millions of dollars on **advertising**. They want you to buy their products and use their **services**, and they want you to remember their company name. Companies use color so that you will **notice** them and so that you will think about them when you see their colors. One research project showed that color helps people remember company names. Colors are very important to businesses.

2   Blue is often used by computer companies. Microsoft and Dell use the color blue to show that their companies are serious and **dependable**. Like the sky and the ocean, blue can be both peaceful and powerful. To show that their computers are for serious people, many companies used to make their computers black or gray. But Apple decided that they wanted computers to be fun instead of serious. For that reason, they made their iMac computers in a variety of different colors in the late 1990s. Today, their computers, laptops, and cell phones come in a variety of colors.

3   BP uses green and yellow for its colors. It is the only large oil company to use green. Green is the color of nature. Yellow is the color of the sun. Both colors are bright and cheerful. BP hopes that people will think of it as a friendly company. In addition, green may make you think of the **environment**. BP wants people to think of it as a company that cares about the environment.

4   United Parcel Service (UPS) is a large delivery company. Its company color is brown. When UPS started in the 1920s, brown was a good color for a safe, reliable company. From the beginning, UPS used brown trucks and brown uniforms. In today's world, brown may seem like a boring color choice for a company. But UPS decided to make it a positive symbol of its business. Their ads ask, "What can brown do for you?" When people see the big brown UPS trucks, the company hopes they will think of excellent, dependable service.

A UPS truck and delivery person

5   All over the world, companies use color to **establish** their brand[1] and to **encourage** people to buy their products. Companies believe that customers respond strongly to their colors. It isn't surprising that companies carefully **consider** the colors for their products and their advertising.

[1] **brand:** the name of a product that is made by a specific company

B. IDENTIFY Check (✓) the main idea of the article.

_____ 1. Companies don't care if you remember their colors, as long as you buy their products.

_____ 2. Companies use color, so you will notice them and remember their company when you see their colors.

_____ 3. Blue is a good color for computer companies.

_____ 4. Many companies use green because it shows they care about the environment.

C. CATEGORIZE Complete the chart with information from the article.

Name of company	Company colors	Feelings that colors give
McDonald's	red and yellow	bright, cheerful
		dependable, peaceful, powerful
	variety of colors	
BP		
	brown	

D. COMPOSE Write one or two sentences to describe each company, its colors, and the meaning of the colors. Use your answers from Activity C.

1. McDonald's: _McDonald's uses red and yellow because they are bright_

and cheerful colors.

2. UPS: _____

3. computer companies: _____

4. BP: _____

CRITICAL THINKING STRATEGY

Restating

A good way to see if you understand an idea is to **restate** it. When you restate something, you write or say the idea using different words. If you repeat something exactly, it isn't always clear that you understand it. To restate the idea, you need to show that you understand what it means. When you restate, be sure not to use exactly the same language.

Original Statement	Restatement (using different words)
Every year, large companies spend millions of dollars on advertising.	Each year big companies use a lot of money to tell people about their products and services.
All over the world, companies use color to establish their brand and to encourage people to buy their products.	In many places, businesses use color, so people will know who they are and buy the things they make.

iQ PRACTICE Go online to watch the Critical Thinking Video and check your comprehension. *Practice ⟩ Unit 2 ⟩ Activity 8*

E. RESTATE Restate these sentences. Use different words and language to express the same idea.

1. Research studies show that yellow makes you feel happier.

   _____

2. We think carefully about color when we choose our clothes.

   _____

3. People who like to wear orange are cheerful and enjoy change.

   _____

4. There are not many colors with universal meaning.

   _____

5. In today's world, brown may seem like a boring color choice for a company.

   _____

F. APPLY Complete each statement with a word from the box. Use the context in the reading to help you understand each word.

cheerful	positive	products	reliable	respond

1. Red, yellow, and green are examples of _____ colors.

2. UPS wants customers to see them as a dependable company. In other words, customers should think UPS is _____.

3. Some people think that brown is boring, which is negative. UPS has made brown a _____ symbol.

4. Some of the _____ in the article are computers, cell phones, and oil.

5. When customers _____ to a company's colors, they remember the brand and the products.

WORK WITH THE VIDEO

VIDEO VOCABULARY

reflect (v.) to show or express something

inspire (v.) to give somebody the idea for something

build (v.) to become greater in amount or number; to increase

nature (n.) all the plants, animals, etc. in the universe and all the things that happen in it that are not made or caused by people

skin tone (n.) one of the shades of the color of people's skin

A. PREVIEW Do you have a favorite color? What is it? How does it make you feel?

iQ RESOURCES   Go online to watch the video about color.
Resources › Video › Unit 2 › Unit Video

B. IDENTIFY Watch the video two or three times. Then choose the correct answer.

1. Pantone has chosen a Color of the Year for ____ years.

   a. 20   b. 17   c. 7

2. The Color of the Year inspires ____.

   a. fashion trends   b. how people feel   c. society

3. The Color of the Year for 2017 is ____.

   a. Lemon yellow   b. Blue   c. Greenery

4. This is a good color because it connects us to ____.

   a. the natural world   b. beauty   c. pop culture

C. EXTEND Think about the different colors people are wearing in your classroom. Do you notice any trends or patterns?

WRITE WHAT YOU THINK

SYNTHESIZE Think about Reading 1, Reading 2, and the unit video as you discuss these questions. Then choose one question and write a response.

WRITING TIP

When you describe a business and its colors, use the simple present. Also use the simple present to give your own opinion. Check that each sentence has a subject and a verb.

1. Think of a company or service that you are familiar with. What colors does it use for its products and advertising? Why do you think the company chose those colors?

2. Imagine that you are going to design a reading room for children. What colors would you use for the tables and shelves, for the walls, and for a reading area? Why would you use those colors?

VOCABULARY SKILL   Suffixes

A **suffix** is a letter or group of letters at the end of a word. A suffix changes the form of a word. Common suffixes for changing a noun to an adjective are *–ful* and *–al*.

Nathaniel's favorite **color** is purple.
noun

Elizabeth loved to plant **colorful** flowers.
adjective

The researcher finished the **experiment** in one month.
noun

The tests were **experimental**, and they didn't prove anything.
adjective

Understanding suffixes can help you increase your vocabulary. If you know the meaning of a noun, then you may be able to also understand its adjective form.

Noun	Adjective	Noun	Adjective
cheer	cheerful	education	educational
joy	joyful	nation	national

Sometimes when you add a suffix, there are spelling changes to the noun form.

Noun	Adjective	Noun	Adjective
biology	biological	finance	financial

A. IDENTIFY Read each sentence. Write *N* (noun) or *ADJ* (adjective) for each bold word.

_N_ 1. Martin left his restaurant in his son's **care**.

____ 2. Laura was **careful** when she chose a company logo.

____ 3. The color green is a **universal** symbol of nature.

____ 4. Kathryn feels small when she thinks about how big the **universe** is.

_____ 5. **Psychology** was Mary's favorite subject in college.

_____ 6. The doctor was worried about Alan's **psychological** problems.

_____ 7. The president greeted the king with a **respectful** bow.

_____ 8. The new police officer quickly won the **respect** of the local residents.

B. CATEGORIZE Complete the chart with the correct form of each word. Then check your answers in the dictionary.

TIP FOR SUCCESS

When you learn a new word, look in the dictionary for its other forms such as noun, verb, adjective, and adverb. This is an easy way to expand your vocabulary.

Nouns	Adjectives
1. addition	additional
2. environment	
3. nature	
4.	peaceful
5.	personal

C. APPLY Complete the paragraph with a noun or adjective from Activity B.

Many people don't like running because they think it's difficult, but I really enjoy it. I usually run in a beautiful park near my house. There are lots of trees and birds in the park. I like running there because I like _____. The park is far away from the noise of the city, so it's very quiet and _____. Some people prefer to run with another _____, but I prefer to run alone, especially before work. My job is stressful, but running helps me feel more relaxed. I enjoy being out in the natural _____. I usually run three miles every morning, but sometimes I have time for a(n) _____ mile or two. Maybe someday I'll run ten miles!

iQ PRACTICE Go online for more practice with suffixes. *Practice > Unit 2 > Activity 9*

WRITING

OBJECTIVE ▶

At the end of this unit, you will write a proposal for a new business. In your proposal, you will choose the colors for the business and explain why you chose these colors. This proposal will include specific information from the readings and your own ideas.

WRITING SKILL Brainstorming

Brainstorming is a way to get ideas before you write. When you brainstorm, you write down ideas quickly. Here are three useful ways to brainstorm.

Listing is a way to quickly write down ideas related to your topic. For example, if your topic is what the color white represents in your culture, you might write a quick list with ideas such as *goodness, cleanliness,* and *freshness*.

Making **idea maps** can also help you brainstorm. Write a keyword in a center circle. Then write related words around the keyword.

In **freewriting**, you give yourself five or ten minutes to write down all of your thoughts about a topic. Freewriting helps you think freely and creatively.

Here are some tips for brainstorming.

- Write down every idea that comes to you for five or ten minutes.
- Don't worry about whether an idea is a good one or not.
- Try to stay focused and write only about your topic.
- When you finish, look at your ideas. Choose the best ideas to develop for your writing.

A. APPLY Read the topic and questions below. Then list ideas that will help you with the topic.

Topic: Think of your favorite color. What items do you have in that color? Why do you like the color? How does it make you feel?

_____   _____

_____   _____

_____   _____

_____   _____

B. APPLY Read the topic below. Write each color in the center circle. Then add ideas around each color to make idea maps.

Topic: Think of a national flag. What are the main colors in the flag? What does each color represent?

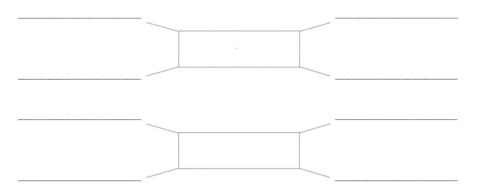

C. WRITING MODEL Read the freewriting example. Cross out information that does not focus on the topic. Compare your answers with a partner.

Topic: How do companies use color to advertise their products? Write about companies that use color effectively.

Companies and colors, Internet companies—Google uses lots of different colors, they are bright, happy colors—Amazon uses mostly black and yellow I think. I wonder why they picked those colors. My brother bought a backpack on Amazon. He takes it to school every day. Stores—Macy's department store uses red. I like the color red. It's a strong, exciting color. Macy's uses a red star in its advertisements. I always think of the red star and Macy's. Sometimes I shop at Macy's. The red star is a good symbol. It's easy to remember and recognize.

D. IDENTIFY Here's the beginning of a paragraph about the topic from Activity C. Underline information in Activity C that can be used in the paragraph.

Macy's and Target, two large department stores, both use the color red in their advertising.

E. CREATE Read the questions below. Then follow the steps to brainstorm and share your ideas.

Topic: Think of a well-known restaurant, clothing store, department store, or company. How does the company use color in their advertising or inside their place of business? How do the colors make you feel?

Steps:

1. First, choose a business to write about. Then brainstorm for five to ten minutes. Use listing, idea maps, or freewriting.

2. After you stop writing, read through your notes. Underline the ideas you want to use in your writing.

3. Share your brainstorming with your partner. Explain your ideas and answer any questions.

F. CREATE Write a paragraph about the topic. Use your brainstorming notes and any new ideas.

iQ PRACTICE Go online for more practice with brainstorming.
Practice > Unit 2 > Activity 10

GRAMMAR Future with *will*

In academic writing, use the future with *will* for predictions about the future and to express what experts predict.

- The designer **will establish** a second office in a new location.
- There **will be** a survey asking about the best color for the new library.

Note: You can soften a prediction by using *probably*. You can also use *may* instead of the future with *will*.

- The designer **will <u>probably</u> establish** a second office in a new location.
- The designer **<u>may</u> establish** a second office in a new location.

Use the future with *will* to make a promise.

- I **will help** you in about an hour.

Use the future with *will* to express plans in more formal writing.

- Next month we **will decide on** new colors for the kitchen.

Use the future with *will* to express a decision made at the moment of writing.

- I**'ll go** to the meeting with you.

Note: Use the future with *be going to* to express a decision or plans that you made previously. This form is more common in informal speaking and writing.

- I **am going to have** dinner with my cousin.

iQ RESOURCES Go online to watch the Grammar Skill Video.
Resources > Video > Unit 2 > Grammar Skill Video

A. APPLY Complete the paragraphs with the future with *will*.

Every year, the biggest paint companies introduce their newest "color of the year." Last week, companies announced their new colors, and designers are very excited about them. These wonderful new paints _____ available

1. be
in January of next year.

"Beautiful Breeze" is a gentle, soft blue. This color _____

2. encourage
comfort and simple designs. Designers _____ this color with

3. use
silver or white. It _____ also _____ well with

4. go
warm browns.

"Garden Pool" is a combination of natural green and quiet blue. Next year, this cool color _____ probably _____ a big hit.

5. be
Customers _____ this deep color. They _____

6. love   7. enjoy
combining it with natural colors like beige or brown.

"Sunflower" is an energetic yellow. In the home, it _____

8. bring
a natural energy and warmth. Homeowners _____ likely

_____ it with calm greens and light browns.

9. use

However you use color, next year you _____ a wide variety

10. have
of color choices. These color trends _____ homes a fresh and

11. offer
modern feeling.

B. EXTEND Look back at the first paragraph in Activity A. Find the verbs. Complete the chart with verbs from the paragraph and the reason each verb form was used.

	Example	Reason
1. simple present	introduce	
2. simple past		
3. future with *will*		

C. COMPOSE Answer the questions about your city or town and yourself. Use the future with *will*.

1. How will your city or town be different in 50 years?

   _____

2. How will transportation be different?

   _____

3. What will stores be like?

   _____

4. In what ways will the environment be different?

   _____

5. How will you be different?

   _____

6. How will your family be different?

   _____

7. What will your job be like?

   _____

iQ PRACTICE   Go online for more practice with the future with *will*.
Practice > Unit 2 > Activities 11–12

UNIT ASSIGNMENT   Write a proposal for a business

OBJECTIVE ▶

In this assignment, you will write a proposal for a new business. Your proposal will include information about what colors you will use and why. As you prepare to write, think about the Unit Question, "How do colors affect our behavior?" Use information from Reading 1, Reading 2, the unit video, and your work in this unit to support your business proposal. Refer to the Self-Assessment checklist on page 48.

iQ PRACTICE   Go online to the Writing Tutor to read a model business proposal.
Practice > Unit 2 > Activity 13

PLAN AND WRITE

A. BRAINSTORM Choose a business. Your new business could sell a product such as clothing, computers, or a type of food. Or your business could be a service such as a restaurant, repair shop, school, airline, or health service.

B. PLAN Freewrite ideas about your new business.

1. Think about these questions as you freewrite.
   - What is the name of your business?
   - What kind of business is it?
   - What colors do you want to use for your business and your advertisements?
   - Why do you want to use these colors?
   - How do you want these colors to make your customers feel?

2. Discuss your ideas with a partner. Answer any questions your partner has about your ideas. Decide which ideas are the best.

iQ PRACTICE Go online to download and complete the outline for your business proposal. *Resources > Writing Tools > Unit 2 > Outline*

C. WRITE Use your planning notes to write your paragraph.

iQ PRACTICE Go online to the Writing Tutor to write your assignment. *Practice > Unit 2 > Activity 14*

1. Complete your new business proposal. Fill out the top part of the form. Then write a paragraph to explain your plan. Use the future with *will* when appropriate.

2. Look at the Self-Assessment checklist on page 48 to guide your writing.

New Business Proposal

Company name: _____

Product or service: _____

Main colors (two or three): _____

Reason for choosing these colors:

_____

_____

REVISE AND EDIT

iQ RESOURCES Go online to download the peer review worksheet.
Resources > Writing Tools > Unit 2 > Peer Review Worksheet

A. PEER REVIEW Read your partner's proposal. Then use the peer review worksheet. Discuss the review with your partner.

B. REWRITE Based on your partner's review, revise and rewrite your proposal.

C. EDIT Complete the Self-Assessment checklist as you prepare to write the final draft of your proposal. Be prepared to hand in your work or discuss it in class.

SELF-ASSESSMENT	Yes	No
Do all of your ideas focus on the topic of your proposal?	☐	☐
Do you use the future with *will* correctly?	☐	☐
Do you use any adjectives with suffixes? Do you use the correct suffixes?	☐	☐
Does the proposal include vocabulary from this unit?	☐	☐
Did you check the proposal for punctuation, spelling, and grammar?	☐	☐

D. REFLECT Discuss these questions with a partner or group.

1. What is something new you learned in this unit?

2. Look back at the Unit Question—How do colors affect our behavior?
   Is your answer different now than when you started the unit? If yes, how is it different? Why?

iQ PRACTICE Go to the online discussion board to discuss the questions.
Practice > Unit 2 > Activity 15

"The Gates" public art installation by artists Christo
and Jean-Claude in Central Park, New York, the United States

TRACK YOUR SUCCESS

iQ PRACTICE Go online to check the words and phrases you have learned in this unit. *Practice › Unit 2 › Activity 16*

Check (✓) the skills you learned. If you need more work on a skill, refer to the page(s) in parentheses.

READING	☐ I can get meaning from context. (p. 33)
CRITICAL THINKING	☐ I can restate an idea. (p.38)
VOCABULARY	☐ I can use suffixes to change word forms. (p. 40)
WRITING	☐ I can brainstorm in three different ways. (p.42)
GRAMMAR	☐ I can use the future with *will* correctly in sentences. (p. 44)

OBJECTIVE ▶   ☐ I can gather information and ideas to write a proposal that explains the colors I will use for a new business.

Social Psychology

3

READING identifying supporting details
VOCABULARY prefixes
WRITING supporting your main idea with examples
GRAMMAR subject-verb agreement
CRITICAL THINKING organizing ideas with a rough outline

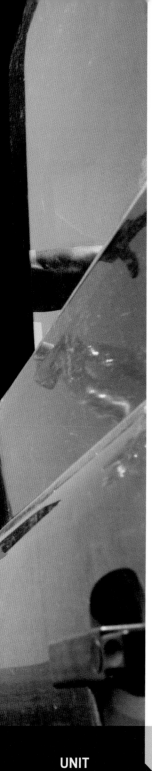

What does it mean to be polite?

A Discuss these questions with your classmates.

1. Describe a time when someone was rude to you. What happened? What did you do?

2. Look at the photo. What is the woman doing? What do you think of her behavior?

B Listen to *The Q Classroom* online. Then answer these questions.

1. What examples do the students give of polite behavior?

2. Can you think of a situation when you tried to be polite but someone misunderstood you?

iQ PRACTICE Go to the online discussion board to discuss the Unit Question with your classmates. *Practice > Unit 3 > Activity 1*

UNIT OBJECTIVE ▶ Read the articles. Gather information and ideas to write a paragraph in response to a question on an online discussion board.

Being Polite from Culture to Culture

OBJECTIVE ▶

You are going to read an article from a travel magazine about being polite in different cultures. Use the article to gather information and ideas for your Unit Assignment.

PREVIEW THE READING

A. VOCABULARY Here are some words from Reading 1. Read the sentences. Then write each underlined word next to the correct definition.

1. I had an <u>awkward</u> conversation with my friend about money. He always borrows money and forgets to repay me.

2. Sam has really bad <u>manners</u>. He never says "please" or "thank you" to anyone, and he often talks with food in his mouth.

3. The boys dressed <u>appropriately</u> for the wedding. They wore nice suits.

4. Psychologists are interested in human <u>behavior</u>. They are studying what people do in different situations.

5. When the president entered the room, everyone stood up as a sign of <u>respect</u>.

6. Nat held his daughter's hand <u>firmly</u> when they crossed the street. He wanted to make sure she walked next to him.

7. When you have a job interview, it's important to <u>make a good impression</u>. You should dress well, arrive on time, and ask questions.

8. Laura made a <u>gesture</u> to ask the waiter to bring the check because she didn't want to shout across the restaurant.

a. _____ (*noun*) polite behavior toward someone or something you think is important

b. _____ (*noun*) the way you act or behave

c. _____ (*adjective*) not comfortable, embarrassing

d. _____ (*verb phrase*) to produce a good effect or opinion

e. _____ (*adverb*) in a strong, steady way

f. _____ (*noun*) ways of acting that are considered polite in your society or culture

g. _____ (*adverb*) suitable or right for a particular situation

h. _____ (*noun*) a movement of the hand or head to express something

iQ PRACTICE Go online for more practice with the vocabulary.
Practice > Unit 3 > Activities 2–3

B. PREVIEW Look at the photos and the captions in the article. What do they tell you about the topic of the article?

C. QUICK WRITE What are some things that might be considered polite in some cultures but not in others? Write a response before you read the article. If possible, give examples to support your answers. Be sure to use this section for your Unit Assignment.

WORK WITH THE READING

A. INVESTIGATE Read the magazine article and gather information about what it means to be polite.

Being Polite from Culture to Culture

1   Most people want to be polite and behave well around others. Being polite means knowing how to greet and talk to people. It means using good **manners** when eating. It means knowing how to give and receive gifts **appropriately**. Polite **behavior** in one country, however, may be impolite in another part of the world. Travelers need to understand the cultural differences in politeness so that they don't cause embarrassment.

2   For instance, when people meet, they often shake hands. How long should a handshake be? Should you hold the other person's hand gently or **firmly**? In the United States, people prefer to shake hands firmly for a few seconds. In some Middle Eastern countries, people hold the person's hand gently for a longer time. Handshaking varies around the world.

3   What about eye contact[1]? In some countries you show **respect** when you look someone directly in the eye. In other parts of the world, to look at someone directly is rude. To be respectful, a person looks down at the ground.

4   There are also cultural differences in the way people use personal space[2]. When two people are talking, should they stand close together or far apart? Exactly how close should they stand? In North America, for instance, people usually stand about an arm's length apart during a conversation. However, in some countries in the Middle East and Latin America, people stand closer. It can be **awkward** if one person likes to stand close and the other person likes to stand farther apart.

---

[1] **eye contact:** a look directly into someone else's eyes   [2] **personal space:** the area that is close to a person

In some countries, making eye
contact shows respect.

5   Three authors wrote a book *Kiss, Bow, or Shake Hands* about cultural differences. In their book, they discuss greetings, gift-giving, and time. Around the world, cultures have different ideas about giving gifts. In the United States, if someone gives you a gift, you should open it while they are with you. That way they can see how happy you are to receive it. In China, you should open a gift after the person is gone.

6   Another cultural difference is time. If someone invites you to dinner at their house at 6 p.m., what time should you get there? Should you arrive early, late, or exactly on time? In Germany, it is important to arrive on time. In Argentina, polite dinner guests usually come 30 to 60 minutes after the time of the invitation. When traveling, remember that each country has a different definition of being on time.

7   A final area to be careful about is body language, including **gestures**. Is it acceptable to touch a person on the shoulder? How do you wave goodbye or hello? How do you gesture to someone to "come here"? All of these can be different from one culture to another. In Vietnam, it is rude to touch someone on the head with the palm of the hand. The gesture for "come here" in the U.S. is only used for calling animals in some other countries.

Being polite means knowing how to give and receive
gifts appropriately.

8   If you are going to live, work, or study in another country, it is important to learn the language. But it is also important to learn about cultural differences. This way, you can be polite and **make a good impression**. People around you will feel comfortable and respected. Politeness and good manners can be good for making friends, good for traveling, and good for business, too.

B. CATEGORIZE Read the statements. Write *T* (true) or *F* (false). Then correct each false statement to make it true. Write the paragraph number where the answer is found.

____ 1. Polite behavior is the same everywhere.

Paragraph: ____ _____

____ 2. People make eye contact in different ways in different cultures.

Paragraph: ____ _____

____ 3. Most people are comfortable with same amount of personal space.

Paragraph: ____ _____

_____ 4. Being on time is important in every culture.

Paragraph: _____ _____

_____ 5. Some gestures are polite in one country and rude in another.

Paragraph: _____ _____

_____ 6. It's only important to know what is polite in your own country.

Paragraph: _____ _____

C. IDENTIFY Circle the answer to each question.

1. Why do travelers need to understand cultural differences in politeness?

    a. so they will understand the history of the country they are visiting

    b. so no one will be embarrassed

    c. so they will feel better about themselves

2. How do people in the United States prefer to shake hands?

    a. firmly for a short time

    b. gently for a short time

    c. firmly for a long time

3. How closely do people in Latin America or the Middle East like to stand while talking?

    a. at an arm's length

    b. more than an arm's length

    c. less than an arm's length

4. What should you do if someone in China gives you a gift?

    a. open it in front of the person

    b. wait until the person has left before opening it

    c. open the gift immediately

5. You are invited for dinner at 7:00 p.m. in Germany. What time should you arrive?

    a. 6:30 p.m.

    b. 7:00 p.m.

    c. 7:30 p.m.

6. If you show that you understand cultural differences and politeness, how will people feel?

    a. comfortable and respected

    b. uncomfortable and awkward

    c. polite and happy

D. CATEGORIZE Complete the chart. Use countries or regions and topics from the boxes.

Countries / Regions

Argentina	Latin America
China	Middle Eastern countries
Germany	North America
United States	
Vietnam	

Topics

gestures	personal space
gift-giving	time
greetings	

Paragraph number	Country or region	Topic
2	United States, Middle Eastern countries	greetings
4		
5		
6		
7		

E. DISCUSS Discuss these questions in a group.

1. What are some examples of what it means to be polite?

2. In what ways is shaking hands different in different parts of the world?

3. What is the comfortable distance for conversation in North America? Is it the same where you live?

4. How does being polite help you make a good impression?

iQ PRACTICE Go online for additional reading and comprehension.
Practice > Unit 3 > Activity 4

WRITE WHAT YOU THINK

A. EXTEND Ask and answer the questions with a partner.

1. How would you describe your culture's use of personal space to a foreign visitor? Include space in public spaces, in school, and at work.

2. How do children learn to be polite?

B. **CREATE** Choose one of the questions in Activity A on page 56 and write a response. Use supporting examples. Look back at your Quick Write on page 53 as you think about what you learned.

Question: _____

My response: _____

_____

_____

_____

READING SKILL Identifying supporting details

A well-written article includes **details** that support the main ideas. Details can be facts, reasons, or examples. Identifying supporting details will help you understand the main ideas of an article.

Main Idea	Bowing is a form of greeting in many countries.	
Supporting Details	**fact:** something you know is true	Bowing is the traditional greeting in East Asia.
	reason: the cause of something	People bow low when greeting older people because it is a sign of respect.
	example: something that shows what something is like	In a very formal bow, the forehead sometimes touches the floor.

Identifying and underlining important supporting details as you read can help you improve your reading comprehension.

A. **IDENTIFY** Reread paragraph 4 in Reading 1. Look at the main idea of the paragraph. Write two details that support it. Then compare your answers with a partner.

_____

_____

B. **IDENTIFY** Reread paragraph 5. Answer the questions. Then compare your answers with a partner.

1. What is the main idea? _____

2. How many supporting details are in the paragraph? What are they?

_____

_____

C. IDENTIFY Reread paragraph 6. Answer the questions. Then compare your answers with a partner.

1. What is the main idea? _____

2. What examples does the writer use as supporting details?

_____

_____

iQ PRACTICE Go online for more practice with identifying supporting details. *Practice > Unit 3 > Activity 5*

READING 2

OBJECTIVE ▶

Answers to All Your Travel Questions

You are going to read an online discussion board with questions and advice about customs in different countries. Use the posts to gather information and ideas for your Unit Assignment.

PREVIEW THE READING

TIP FOR SUCCESS
In Unit 2, you learned about using suffixes to expand vocabulary. Add the suffixes *–ful* or *–al* to the following nouns to change them to adjectives: *respect, culture, tradition.* Use your dictionary to check spelling.

A. VOCABULARY Here are some words from Reading 2. Read the sentences. Circle the answer that best matches the meaning of each underlined word or phrase.

1. My uncle gave me some good <u>advice</u> about starting a business.

   a. money that someone loans you

   b. proverbs or famous quotes

   c. words that help someone decide what to do

2. A <u>custom</u> you will notice when you go to Japan is that people don't wear their shoes inside their homes.

   a. way of doing things

   b. thing for sale

   c. idea

3. It's rude to <u>interrupt</u> someone when they are speaking. You should always let them finish.

   a. make someone stop talking

   b. repeat something over and over

   c. whisper; talk quietly

4. I want to <u>take part in</u> the meeting about the neighborhood school. I think it's going to be very interesting.

   a. divide up; separate

   b. join, participate in

   c. act in

5. Classes at many universities are <u>informal</u>. Students can bring food to class and ask questions whenever they want.

   a. lengthy; taking a long time

   b. relaxed and friendly

   c. useful and informative

6. It's <u>traditional</u> in some countries for the bride to wear a white dress for the wedding. In other countries the bride wears red.

   a. inexpensive

   b. doing what others want you to do

   c. ways of doing things that have existed for a long time

7. Try to <u>avoid</u> talking when you have food in your mouth. It's very rude!

   a. choose not to

   b. adjust

   c. continue

8. On a <u>typical</u> day, Erik works from 9:00 a.m. to 5:00 p.m., but today he worked until 7:30 p.m.

   a. pleasant

   b. awkward

   c. usual

iQ PRACTICE Go online for more practice with the vocabulary.
Practice > Unit 3 > Activities 6–7

B. PREVIEW In this online discussion board, travelers ask for advice about customs in different countries. What kinds of topics do you think the travelers will ask about?

☐ greeting people   ☐ giving/receiving gifts

☐ conversation topics   ☐ table manners

☐ other _____

WRITING TIP
When you are freewriting, remember to write whatever ideas come to you. You can improve and revise your ideas later.

C. QUICK WRITE Choose one of the topics in Activity B. What are some of the customs in your country? What about in other countries? Write a few sentences. Be sure to use this section for your Unit Assignment.

WORK WITH THE READING

 A. INVESTIGATE Read the posts from the online discussion board and gather information about what it means to be polite.

Sign in

| Home | About | Contact | Forum |

ANSWERS TO ALL YOUR TRAVEL QUESTIONS

Yong Jun Park, Seoul Posted: 3 days ago	**Question: First trip to U.S.** For my new job, I will travel to the United States next month and meet my American boss. This will be my first trip to the U.S. I'm worried about correct business etiquette[1] and manners. My boss invited me to her family's home for dinner. Do you have any **advice**?
Sue, Miami Posted: 3 days ago	**1. Re: First trip to U.S.** It's a good idea to bring a small gift or something from your country. Don't be surprised if your boss opens the gift right away. In the U.S., people often open a gift when they receive it. In Korea, that is not polite, but it's appropriate in the U.S.
Jun, Seoul Posted: 2 days ago	**2. Re: First trip to U.S.** Most Americans are very **informal** at home. One time I went to dinner at the home of an American business partner. I was surprised that everyone stood and talked in the kitchen while the husband and wife cooked dinner. Also, unlike in Korea, everyone **took part in** the dinner table conversation, even the man's wife and children.
Andrea, Santiago Posted: 12 hours ago	**3. Re: First trip to U.S.** I agree with Jun. I was surprised that American men often cook and that both the husband and wife come to the dinner table and talk. You probably won't speak about business during dinner, so my advice is to know some good topics of conversation. For example, you can talk about travel, food, or sports. Of course, it's good to ask about your boss's family. But it's not polite to ask questions about age, salary, religion, or politics.
Sun Hee Choi, Pusan Posted: 8 hours ago	**4. Re: First trip to U.S.** Americans use their hands to eat some kinds of food, such as pizza and fried chicken. Watch your American hosts[2], and do what they do.
Kathryn, New York Posted: 5 hours ago	**5. Re: First trip to U.S.** In Korea and Japan, it's the **custom** to remove your shoes before entering a house. In the United States, you usually don't take your shoes off. Once I was traveling in Japan and entered a house with my shoes on by mistake. Oops!
Yong Jun Park, Seoul Posted: 2 hours ago	**6. Re: First trip to U.S.** It sounds like Americans are so informal. I'll try to be informal and polite. I hope I do the right thing. Thanks for all the advice! One more question: What's an appropriate gift for me to bring my boss and her family?

[1] **etiquette:** polite and correct behavior in a social situation
[2] **hosts:** people who have visitors to the home and entertain them

Sam, Los Angeles Posted: 4 days ago	**Question: Travel to Egypt** Any tips on table manners in Egypt? I'll be there on business, and I'm sure we will have business dinners. Also, anything else that's important to know?
Khalid, Cairo Posted: 12 hours ago	**1. Re: Travel to Egypt** Egypt is a **traditional** country, and it has many customs that are different from the U.S. Table manners are similar to the U.S., but there are a few important differences. For instance, it's impolite to use your left hand to eat. Be sure to read about Egyptian culture before you go. You can **avoid** embarrassing yourself.
Carlos, Madrid Posted: 2 hours ago	**2. Re: Travel to Egypt** I traveled to Egypt on business last year and saw two interesting differences in business. First, unlike Americans, Egyptians don't discuss business at the beginning of business meetings. Instead they begin with informal conversation. This is because personal relationships are very important in Egyptian business. Second, during a meeting in Egypt, it's common for others to come in the room and **interrupt** the meeting. In the United States, it's rude to interrupt a meeting. In Egypt, these interruptions are **typical**!

B. CATEGORIZE Read the false statements. Correct them to make them true. Write the name of the person who posted the correct information.

1. Yong Jun Park's host will probably talk about business during dinner.

   Name: _____

2. It is appropriate to bring a large gift when visiting a home in the U.S.

   Name: _____

3. Many Americans are very formal at home.

   Name: _____

4. In Egypt, it is rude to come in and interrupt a business meeting.

   Name: _____

C. IDENTIFY Write information from the online discussion board for each of the topics below.

1. when to open gifts

   a. in South Korea _____

   b. in the U.S. _____

2. conversation topics in the U.S.

    a. good topics _____

    b. impolite topics _____

3. beginning business meetings

    a. in the U.S. _____

    b. in Egypt _____

4. interruptions in business meetings

    a. in Egypt _____

    b. in the U.S. _____

D. APPLY Complete the sentences with words from the box.

conversation	informal	kitchen	manners	relationships
hosts	interrupt	left	polite	

Some people who travel are worried about etiquette
and _____ because customs may be
              1
different in another country. For example, most Americans are

_____ at home. It isn't unusual for conversations
         2
to take place in the _____ while preparing a
                        3
meal. Travel, food, or sports are _____ topics for
                                   4
conversation. If you aren't sure what to do when eating, you can watch your

_____.
         5

If you travel to Egypt, you should be careful not to eat with your

_____ hand. At business meetings in Egypt,
         6
it is common to begin with informal _____
                                 7
because personal _____ are important in
                      8
Egyptian business. You should also expect to have people come in and

_____ the meeting while it is taking place.
         9

E. DISCUSS Discuss these questions with a partner or in a group.

1. What are some examples of good table manners?

2. If guests from another country visit you, should they adapt to the behavior in your culture, or should you try to make them feel at home by doing things their way?

WORK WITH THE VIDEO

A. PREVIEW Is it polite to use a mobile phone in a restaurant? Why? Why not?

VIDEO VOCABULARY

emerge (v.) to come out from somewhere; to become known

chat (v.) to talk to someone in a friendly, informal way

invade (v.) to come in and disturb

ban (v.) to officially say that something is not allowed

iQ RESOURCES Go online to watch the video about mobile phones.
Resources > Video > Unit 3 > Unit Video

B. CATEGORIZE Watch the video two or three times. Write *T* (true) or *F* (false) for each statement.

1. What is polite is the same across different cultures. ____

2. In the U.S., most people think it is rude to talk on your phone at a family dinner. ____

3. In Japan, it is acceptable to talk on a mobile phone on a train. ____

4. In China, it is rude to interrupt a conversation to answer the phone. ____

5. France has banned mobile phones from schools. ____

C. DISCUSS Discuss the questions with a group.

1. What are some other places where it is acceptable or unacceptable to use a mobile phone? For example, is it acceptable to use a phone during a music concert?

2. Is it ever appropriate to use a phone in a classroom? What rules for phone use can you suggest?

WRITE WHAT YOU THINK

SYNTHESIZE Think about Reading 1, Reading 2, and the unit video as you discuss these questions. Then choose one question and write a response.

1. Do you think that people today are less polite than in the past? Why?

2. Do you think that people are naturally polite? Or do they learn to be polite? Explain.

VOCABULARY SKILL Prefixes

TIP FOR SUCCESS

Not every word starting with *in-*, *im-*, or *un-* has a prefix meaning *not*. For example, these words do not have negative prefixes: *interrupt*, *impression*, *uncle*.

A **prefix** is a group of letters at the beginning of a word. Adding a prefix to a word changes its meaning. Understanding prefixes will help you increase your vocabulary. The prefixes *in-*, *im-*, and *un-* mean *not* and are added to adjectives.

There are no rules for when to use *in-* or *un-*. You need to learn these words or use a dictionary to help you.

| **in**formal | not formal | **un**able | not able |
| **in**visible | not visible | **un**usual | not usual |

Im- is added to an adjective that starts with *m* or *p*.

| **im**mature | not mature |
| **im**polite | not polite |

A. APPLY Look at the words below. Add the correct prefix to each word. Then write the new words in the chart. Check your answers in a dictionary.

appropriate ✓	common	formal	possible
clear	dependable	perfect	traditional
comfortable	expensive	polite	usual

in-	im-	un-
inappropriate		

B. APPLY Complete the sentences with words from Activity A on page 64. Use the word with or without the prefix. For some sentences, there is more than one correct answer.

1. My brother is very _____. He always does what he says he will do.

2. The directions were confusing and _____. Kenan got lost three times trying to get to the restaurant.

3. Because her first name was so _____, she always had to repeat it several times.

4. It's _____ for me to finish the project on time. I have too much research to do. I can't do it.

5. Our receptionist is very friendly and welcoming. She makes people feel _____ when they come into the office.

6. Although it was a small and _____ gift, it was very thoughtful. The cost wasn't important.

7. The customer was very _____. He was so rude that no one wanted to help him.

8. Many people send quick email invitations to celebrations, but Jamal sent a _____ invitation to his graduation in the mail. He chose very expensive paper.

9. The bed was very _____, so I barely slept all night and I had a backache in the morning.

10. In the U.S. it's _____ to ask how old people are or how much money they make.

iQ PRACTICE Go online for more practice with prefixes.
Practice > Unit 3 > Activity 8

WRITING

OBJECTIVE ▶   At the end of this unit, you will write a paragraph in response to a question from an online discussion board. This paragraph will include specific examples from the readings and your own ideas.

WRITING SKILL Supporting your main idea with examples

When you write a paragraph, support your main idea with **examples**. Examples will make your ideas clear to your readers.

Writers often introduce examples with the phrases *for example* and *for instance*.

> My advice is to know good topics of conversation. For example, you can talk about travel, food, or sports.

A. WRITING MODEL Read this model response to Yong Jun Park's question from Reading 2, *What's an appropriate gift for me to bring my boss and her family?* Circle the main idea of the response. Underline the examples. Then highlight any words that the writer uses to introduce examples.

It's difficult to select the right gift to bring a host, especially if you don't know the person or the culture very well. However, there are several appropriate gifts to bring a host. For example, you can bring flowers. Buy a nice bouquet of flowers from a florist or even at the supermarket. Be sure to take the price tag off though. Food is another good example of an appropriate item to bring. Ask the host what you can bring, or bring something everybody will probably enjoy, like a basket of fruit. If you don't want to bring food or flowers, be creative. For instance, you can bring a small gift for the home. Think of something that people use even if they already have it. Soap and hand towels are a good idea.

B. RESTATE Complete the sentences. Use information from Reading 1 and Reading 2.

1. The idea of personal space is different from one country to another.

   For example, _____

2. In the United States, you should shake hands firmly. This is not true everywhere, however. For instance, _____

3. In Latin America, people don't always arrive exactly on time. For instance,

   _____

4. In many Asian countries it is rude to open a gift right away. However, in some countries you should open a gift immediately. For example,

_____

5. The idea of politeness can vary from one country to another. For instance,

_____

C. **CREATE** Read the main idea and supporting detail in the chart below. Then add more supporting ideas.

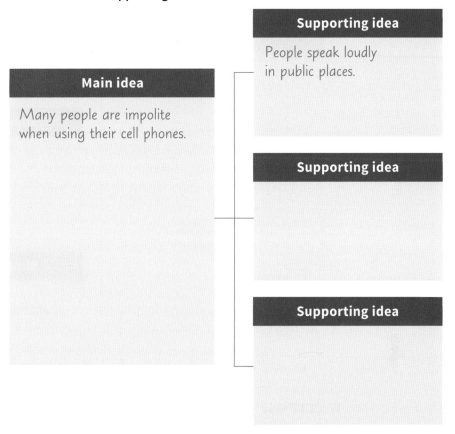

D. **COMPOSE** Copy the topic and concluding sentences below. Then complete the paragraph. Give examples to support the main idea in the topic sentence. Use the information from the chart in Activity C.

Topic sentence: Many people do not have good cell phone manners, and they are impolite when they use their phones. For example,. . .

Concluding sentence: . . .If cell phone users were more thoughtful of others, they might be more polite.

ACADEMIC LANGUAGE

As well as *for example* and *for instance*, you can use the phrase *is an example of* in academic writing. *Helping with the housework is an example of how children can show respect for their parents.*

⏋ OPAL
Oxford Phrasal Academic Lexicon

E. CREATE Choose one of the topics below. Then use the chart to show your main idea and two or three examples giving short answers.

Topic A: Do you think it is important for children to show respect for their parents? What are some ways they can do this?

Topic B: Should you study the customs of another country before you visit? What are some things you should learn before traveling to another country?

F. COMPOSE Write a complete paragraph giving examples. Use your notes from Activity E.

1. Write a topic sentence introducing your idea. Make it clear which topic you chose in Activity E.

_____

2. Write two to three supporting sentences introducing examples.

_____

_____

_____

iQ PRACTICE Go online for more practice with supporting your main idea with examples. *Practice › Unit 3 › Activity 9*

GRAMMAR Subject-verb agreement

It is important to make sure that the subject and verb in a sentence agree. Use the singular form of the verb with singular subjects.

My **aunt** always **speaks** in a very loud voice.
    subject   verb

The **cake is** delicious.
    subject verb

Use the plural form of the verb with plural subjects.

Articles about business etiquette **are** very useful.
  subject   verb

My **cats eat** twice a day.
  subject verb

With *there is/there are*, the subject comes after the verb.

There **is** a lot of **information** on the Internet about manners.
  verb   subject

There **are** 15 **students** in my class.
  verb   subject

Remember that some plural nouns do not end in *-s*. For example, *people*, *children*, *police*.

Children learn manners from their parents.
  subject   verb

iQ RESOURCES Go online to watch the Grammar Skill Video.
Resources > Video > Unit 3 > Grammar Skill Video

TIP FOR SUCCESS
When you edit your own writing, circle subjects and underline verbs in every sentence to check for subject-verb agreement.

A. APPLY Circle the subject in each sentence. Then complete the sentence with the correct form of the verb. The first one has been done for you.

1. My (brother) lives_____ (live) in Boston.

2. There _____ (be) a man waiting outside for Paulo.

3. The police in my neighborhood _____ (be) very helpful.

4. People _____ (use) the Internet to get all kinds of information.

5. This book _____ (give) helpful advice on business travel.

B. IDENTIFY Read this post from a website. Circle the subject and underline the verb in each sentence. Then correct the errors in subject-verb agreement.

> In my opinion, the most annoying habit is talking on cell phones. People
>
> is talking on their cell phones all the time. My brother always interrupt our
>
> conversations and answer his phone. People like my brother doesn't care
>
> about manners. People talk on cell phones in restaurants and in doctors'
>
> offices. There is times when cell phones are very annoying. Cell phones ring
>
> and interrupts our thoughts. People need to show more respect for others.
>
> There is appropriate and inappropriate places to use cell phones.

C. IDENTIFY Look back at your paragraph in Activity F on page 68. Check subject-verb agreement. Circle the subject and underline the verb in each sentence.

iQ PRACTICE Go online for more practice with subject-verb agreement. *Practice > Unit 3 > Activities 10–11*

TIP FOR SUCCESS
Uncountable nouns such as *information*, *knowledge*, and *money* require a singular verb.

UNIT ASSIGNMENT Write a paragraph with supporting examples

OBJECTIVE ▶

In this assignment, you will write a paragraph in response to a question posted on an online discussion board about politeness. As you prepare your paragraph, think about the Unit Question, "What does it mean to be polite?" Use information from Reading 1, Reading 2, the unit video, and your work in this unit to support your paragraph. Refer to the Self-Assessment checklist on page 72.

iQ PRACTICE Go online to the Writing Tutor to read a model paragraph with supporting examples. *Practice > Unit 3 > Activity 13*

PLAN AND WRITE

A. BRAINSTORM Read the following questions from an online discussion board. Choose which question you want to answer for your paragraph. Then freewrite your ideas about the question.

1. I'm traveling to the United States for the first time. What do you know about manners in the U.S.? What tips do you have about being polite?

2. I think that people today are very rude. I'm the father of two young boys, ages five and ten. How can I teach my sons to be polite?

CRITICAL THINKING STRATEGY

Organizing ideas with a rough outline

One way to **organize ideas** is to make a rough outline. Write your topic or main idea at the top. Then list your other key ideas below it. For example, if you are giving several tips about being polite, each tip would be a key idea.

Main idea: I have three suggestions about polite manners at a dinner.
Tip: Watch your host or hostess.
Tip: If you need something that is far away, ask someone to pass it to you.
Tip: Always chew with your mouth closed.

After you have done your rough outline, analyze the best order for your points. For example, it is usually better to have your strongest point last. Number your points to show the best order. Here's a possible order:

Tip 1: If you need something that is far away, ask someone to pass it to you.
Tip 2: Always chew with your mouth closed.
Tip 3: Watch your host or hostess.

In a test situation, a rough outline is a good way to quickly organize ideas before you write your answer.

iQ PRACTICE Go online to watch the Critical Thinking Video and check your comprehension. *Practice > Unit 3 > Activity 12*

B. PLAN Complete these activities.

1. Write a topic sentence for your paragraph. Your topic sentence should answer the question you chose and contain your controlling idea.

2. Make a rough outline. List at least three points under your main idea.

3. Discuss your rough outline with a partner. Decide on the best order for your points.

iQ RESOURCES Go online to download and complete the outline for your paragraph with supporting examples.
Resources > Writing Tools > Unit 3 > Outline

C. WRITE Use your planning notes to write your paragraph.

iQ PRACTICE Go online to the Writing Tutor to write your assignment.
Practice > Unit 3 > Activity 14

1. As you write, be sure that your examples support your main idea.

2. Look at the Self-Assessment checklist to guide your writing.

REVISE AND EDIT

iQ RESOURCES Go online to download the peer review worksheet.
Resources > Writing Tools > Unit 3 > Peer Review Worksheet

A. PEER REVIEW Read your partner's paragraph. Then use the peer review worksheet. Discuss the review with your partner.

B. REWRITE Based on your partner's review, revise and rewrite your paragraph.

C. EDIT Complete the Self-Assessment checklist as you prepare to write the final draft of your paragraph. Be prepared to hand in your work or discuss it in class.

SELF-ASSESSMENT	Yes	No
Do all your examples support your main idea?	☐	☐
Do the subjects and verbs agree?	☐	☐
Do you use adjectives with prefixes correctly?	☐	☐
Does your paragraph include vocabulary from this unit?	☐	☐
Did you check the paragraph for punctuation, spelling, and grammar?	☐	☐

D. REFLECT Discuss these questions with a group or partner.

1. What is something new you learned in this unit?

2. Look back at the Unit Question—What does it mean to be polite? Is your answer different now than when you started the unit? If yes, how is it different? Why?

iQ PRACTICE Go to the online discussion board to discuss the questions.
Practice > Unit 3 > Activity 15

TRACK YOUR SUCCESS

iQ PRACTICE   Go online to check the words and phrases you have learned in this unit. *Practice › Unit 3 › Activity 16*

Check (✓) the skills you learned. If you need more work on a skill, refer to the page(s) in parentheses.

READING ☐ I can identify supporting details. (p. 57)

VOCABULARY ☐ I can use prefixes correctly. (p. 64)

WRITING ☐ I can support main ideas with examples. (p. 66)

GRAMMAR ☐ I can use subject-verb agreement correctly. (p. 69)

CRITICAL THINKING ☐ I can organize ideas with a rough outline. (p. 71)

OBJECTIVE ▶ ☐ I can gather information and ideas to write a paragraph in response to a question on an online discussion board.

Technology

4

READING	taking notes
VOCABULARY	using the dictionary
WRITING	writing an opinion paragraph
CRITICAL THINKING	organizing ideas with a graphic organizer
GRAMMAR	modals

How can technology improve performance?

A. Discuss these questions with your classmates.

1. What technology do you use every day? How does it improve your school performance?

2. Look at the photo. What is the girl doing? Where is she and what kind of technology do you think she is using?

B. Listen to *The Q Classroom* online. Then answer these questions.

1. What four examples of technology do the students give?

2. What technology would you like to use to improve performance? How would it help you?

iQ PRACTICE Go to the online discussion board to discuss the Unit Question with your classmates. *Practice > Unit 4 > Activity 1*

UNIT OBJECTIVE

Read the articles. Gather information and ideas to write an opinion paragraph about how to improve performance with technology.

READING

READING 1

Virtual Reality for Medical Students

OBJECTIVE ▶

You are going to read an article about virtual reality in medical school. Use the article to gather information and ideas for your Unit Assignment.

PREVIEW THE READING

A. VOCABULARY Here are some words from Reading 1. Read the sentences. Then write each underlined word or phrase next to the correct definition.

1. A doctor must examine a new patient carefully.

2. After changing her competition music, the ice skater's performance really improved. Her scores were much higher.

3. I need to replace this lamp. The electrical cord is damaged, and it is dangerous.

4. The heavy rain resulted in a dangerous situation by the river.

5. The scientists tested a specific type of plant to see if it could be used as a drug.

6. The day-care workers take care of ten young children each day.

7. Cell phones have new technology so that users can take excellent photos.

8. High school students are under pressure to get high scores on college entrance exams.

ACADEMIC LANGUAGE

As well as *a type of*, the phrase *a kind of* is common in academic writing.

OPAL
Oxford Phrasal Academic Lexicon

---

a. _____ *(adjective)* connected with one particular thing only

b. _____ *(verb)* to be used instead of something else

c. _____ *(noun)* the scientific knowledge or equipment that is needed for a particular industry

d. _____ *(verb)* to study something or someone very carefully

e. _____ *(noun)* things that are happening at a particular time or in a particular place

f. _____ *(verb phrase)* to be responsible for a situation or task

g. _____ *(noun)* how well or badly you do something; how well or badly something works

h. _____ *(prepositional phrase)* made to feel anxious about something you have to do; being forced to do something

iQ PRACTICE Go online for more practice with the vocabulary.
Practice ⟩ Unit 4 ⟩ Activities 2–3

B. PREVIEW Read the title of the article. Read the captions under the photos. What do you know about virtual reality? Have you ever used it?

C. QUICK WRITE How do you use technology to help you learn? Does your school have technology available? What new technology would you like to use? Make a list of all of the technology you can use to learn and study. Remember to use this section for your Unit Assignment.

WORK WITH THE READING

 A. INVESTIGATE Read the article and gather information about how students are learning with virtual reality.

VIRTUAL REALITY FOR MEDICAL STUDENTS

WHAT IS VIRTUAL REALITY?

1   Virtual reality, or VR, is a way to enter into a three-dimensional, computer-generated experience. In two dimensions—for example, in a book—images have length and width, but they have no depth. They appear flat. With VR, you wear special glasses to see the three dimensions, just like in the real world. VR gives you an experience with sight, sound, feeling, and sometimes even smell. With VR, you can move things around as if you are using your hands in the real world. You can make things appear larger or smaller, too.

VIRTUAL REALITY FOR MEDICAL STUDENTS

2   Imagine that you want to become a doctor. You have studied hard for many years, and you have finally gotten into a good medical school. In your first year of medical school, one of your most important courses is anatomy. Anatomy is the study of everything in the human body. For example, you have to learn the name, location, and function of all 206 bones and more than 650 muscles. Would you prefer to learn this by using a book or by using virtual reality?

3   Virtual reality, or VR, is the latest **technology** to help medical students learn about the human body. Usually, students study anatomy by using books. However, books do not show how everything fits together in three dimensions. With VR, students can remove layers of muscles and see how they are connected to bones. They can see how everything fits together. Of course, students still use anatomy textbooks. But, students learn best when they have a variety of ways to learn. VR is giving students a new way to learn anatomy.

4   VR is also giving medical students a new way to practice an important skill: the medical examination. A doctor **examines** a patient and gives a diagnosis[1]. Students learn how to do a medical examination by reading a textbook, watching a doctor, and finally by doing it themselves. But it is a big jump from studying to examining a real patient. With VR, students can practice medical examinations before working with a real patient.

5   Here is how VR is used for learning medical examinations. The instructor chooses the **specific** medical **situation** for the virtual patient. Then the medical student puts on the VR glasses and starts the examination. The student clicks on each part of the body that she needs to check. The VR shows information about the patient. For example, if the student clicks on the eyes, it may say that the eyes are yellow. The student can also have the virtual patient move various body parts. Then the student makes a diagnosis, identifying the problem.

6   When the student finishes, she will get a report on what she did correctly and what she missed in the examination. With VR for medical examinations, students are able to practice many times with virtual patients before examining real patients.

7   One of the most exciting uses of VR in medical education is to practice a much more difficult situation: the hospital emergency room. Doctors are **under** a lot of **pressure**. They have to make life and death decisions quickly. Typically, medical students learn how to perform under pressure only by having experience in an emergency room. But students will not see a great variety of medical situations unless they are there for a long, long time.

8   Fortunately, with VR, students can practice emergency room situations and learn. For example, in one situation, the VR patient may suddenly get a fast heartbeat. The heart monitor[2] changes, and that tells the doctor to do something now or else the patient will be in trouble, explains Dr. Joshua Sherman, an emergency room doctor in Los Angeles. He says that when you take action, you see a change in the VR patient. This "gives you positive reinforcement[3] that you did the correct thing, or the incorrect thing, if the situation gets worse. VR is amazing for that." During the VR experience, students can see the results of their actions.

9   The education of medical students is extremely important because they will be our doctors someday. VR technology can help students improve their **performance** and make them better doctors in the future. Of course, nothing can **replace taking care of** real people in real situations. But, VR can help students practice their skills in new and exciting ways.

[1]**diagnosis:** identification of a problem or illness
[2]**heart monitor:** a piece of equipment to record heartbeats
[3]**positive reinforcement:** process of making it clear that it was a good decision

B. IDENTIFY Circle the main idea of the article.

1. Medical students have a great deal of information to learn.

2. Medical students are learning a variety of skills using virtual reality.

3. Doctors are under a lot of pressure in the emergency room.

4. Virtual reality makes it easier for medical students to learn.

C. IDENTIFY Circle the answer to each question.

1. What is virtual reality?

    a. using special glasses for two dimensions

    b. using technology to feel three dimensions

    c. using computer-generated images

2. What is one of the most important courses in medical school?

    a. human anatomy

    b. medical examinations

    c. emergency room medicine

3. How does a student use VR to do a medical examination?

    a. by watching a doctor

    b. by clicking on parts of the body

    c. by asking the patient to move parts of the body

4. What is a benefit of using VR to practice medical examinations?

    a. students can practice many times before examining a real patient

    b. students can improve their anatomy scores

    c. students can learn how to communicate with patients

5. Why are emergency rooms a difficult situation for students?

    a. the patients have very serious problems

    b. students have to examine real patients

    c. students have to make decisions quickly under pressure

D. EXTEND Answer the questions. Use examples from the reading.

1. How can VR help a student learn and understand anatomy?

   _____

2. Why is it good for medical students to practice medical examinations using VR?

   _____

3. Do you think that practicing emergency room situations using VR is helpful? Why or why not?

   _____

E. SYNTHESIZE Look back at your Quick Write on page 77. Is any of the technology you use similar in any way to virtual reality? For example, does it help you practice certain situations or follow steps in a process? Does it help you learn and identify things? Explain.

iQ PRACTICE   Go online for additional reading and comprehension.
Practice > Unit 4 > Activity 4

? WRITE WHAT YOU THINK

A. DISCUSS Discuss the questions in a group. Think about the Unit Question, How can technology improve performance?

1. How could virtual reality help you in your learning? Give specific examples.

2. Would you like to use virtual reality to learn how to speak English? Why or why not?

B. CREATE Choose one of the questions from Activity A and write a response. Look back at your Quick Write on page 77 as you think about what you learned.

Question: _____

My response: _____

   _____

   _____

   _____

When you read an article or textbook, it is helpful to **take notes** while you read. You can write notes directly in the book next to the text. Taking notes can help you remember what you read. When you take notes, you do not need to write complete sentences. You can write short phrases or even just a few words. You can also underline or highlight important information.

Some things you might note are:

- main ideas
- supporting ideas
- important names, dates, or numbers

You can use your notes for summarizing, answering questions, comparing ideas, or studying for a test.

iQ RESOURCES Go online to watch the Reading Skill Video.
Resources > Video > Unit 4 > Reading Skill Video

A. CATEGORIZE Read the notes in the box. Then write each note in the correct category. Add three more supporting ideas to the chart.

Practice for working under pressure
Student clicks on parts of the body to check
Can see how everything fits together
Students must make decisions quickly
Better way to learn the parts of the body
Can practice before examining a real patient

VR for anatomy
Main idea:
Supporting idea:
Supporting idea:

VR for examinations
Main idea:
Supporting idea:
Supporting idea:

VR for emergency room situations
Main idea:
Supporting idea:
Supporting idea:

iQ PRACTICE Go online for more practice with taking notes.
Practice > Unit 4 > Activity 5

The Technology Advantage

OBJECTIVE ▶

You are going to read an online article about technology in sports. Use the article to gather information and ideas for your Unit Assignment.

PREVIEW THE READING

TIP FOR SUCCESS

Remember to apply what you learned in Unit 3 about using prefixes to expand vocabulary. Add the prefixes *in-*, *im-*, or *un-* to the following words from Readings 1 and 2: *connected, correctly, expensive, happy, important, real*. Use your dictionary to check spelling.

A. VOCABULARY Here are some words from Reading 2. Read their definitions. Then complete each sentence.

advantage *(noun)* 🔑 OPAL something that helps you or is useful

artificial *(adjective)* 🔑 made or produced to copy something natural; not real

ban *(verb)* 🔑 to officially say that something is not allowed

energy *(noun)* 🔑 OPAL strength and ability to be active without getting tired

equipment *(noun)* 🔑 the things that are needed to do a particular activity

invent *(verb)* 🔑 to think of or make something for the first time

reason *(noun)* 🔑 OPAL the cause of something; something that explains why something happens

unfair *(adjective)* 🔑 not treating each person equally

🔑 Oxford 3000™ words   OPAL Oxford Phrasal Academic Lexicon

1. Airline companies agreed to _____ smoking on airplanes many years ago. Now smoking is not allowed on any flights.

2. Playing sports requires a lot of _____, so athletes need to eat healthy foods and drink plenty of water.

3. Many professional sports stadiums have _____ grass, which requires less care and attention than real grass.

4. The _____ for my low test score became clear: I had studied the wrong unit.

5. Ramon is very tall, so he has a(n) _____ when he plays basketball.

6. Running is a popular sport because it is great exercise, and it doesn't require a lot of special _____. All you need are running shoes.

7. My friend is a very creative cook. He likes to _____ new recipes for unusual dishes.

8. The teacher was _____ when she gave additional testing time to some students.

iQ PRACTICE Go online for more practice with the vocabulary.
Practice > Unit 4 > Activities 6–7

B. PREVIEW Preview the reading. Read the first paragraph, the first sentence of each supporting paragraph, and the last paragraph. What would be the best subtitle for the article? Check (✓) your answer.

☐ The Technology Advantage: Computer Companies Support Sports Teams

☐ The Technology Advantage: Improve Your Video Game Skills

☐ The Technology Advantage: Better Equipment, Better Performance

C. QUICK WRITE What are some examples of how technology is improving equipment for athletes? Think, for example, of how technology may improve skis, tennis racquets, or running shoes. Write a few sentences about the topic. Be sure to use this section for your Unit Assignment.

Handwritten annotations: "topic → (circle) words", "quite many ban"

WORK WITH THE READING

 A. INVESTIGATE Read the article and gather information about what makes a competition unfair.

THE TECHNOLOGY ADVANTAGE

Handwritten margin note: "Focus Intro duc tion"

1   Since ancient times, athletes have always looked for ways to win competitions. Athletes can be winners with better training, better coaching, and better food. They can also improve performance with better **equipment**: better shoes, better skis, or a better tennis racquet. Even the early Greeks used engineering to make a better discus[1] to throw. However, people want sports to be fair. For this **reason**, sports organizations make rules about athletes, equipment, and the game itself.

2   Nowadays, new technology is helping athletes. From high-tech clothing to **artificial** arms and legs, there are many new ways to improve performance. However, many people worry that technology can give some athletes an **advantage**. It can make competitions **unfair**. Also, often only wealthier athletes and teams can buy expensive, high-tech equipment. Do we want the best athlete to win or the athlete with the best equipment to win?

3   The story of high-tech swimsuits shows how technology can make sports unfair. Several years ago, sports engineers **invented** a new material for swimsuits. It has many of the same qualities as shark[2] skin. When swimmers use full-body suits made of this material, they swim faster and float better. The material also sends more oxygen to swimmers' muscles.

4   Companies introduced these new high-tech swimsuits in 2008. Soon after, swimmers using the suits began breaking world swim records at a surprising rate. In the 2008 Beijing Olympic Games, swimmers broke 25 world records. Twenty-three of those swimmers wore the high-tech suits. By comparison, Olympic swimmers broke only eight world records in 2004. Then, in the 2009 World Championships, swimmers broke 43 world records. People knew that the new suits were helping athletes. In January 2010, the Fédération Internationale de Natation (International Swimming Federation, or FINA) **banned** the high-tech suits. Most competitive swimmers were happy about the ban. As one Olympic swimmer said, "Swimming is actually swimming again. It's not who's wearing what suit, who has what material. We're all under the same guidelines[3]."

5   In the two years after the ban, swimmers broke only two world records. Clearly the expensive, high-tech suits were the reason behind the faster swimming times. The suits gave some swimmers an unfair advantage.

---

[1] **discus:** a heavy, flat, round object thrown in a sporting event
[2] **shark:** a large, often dangerous, ocean fish with many sharp teeth

[3] **guidelines:** rules or instructions that are given by an official organization telling you how to do something

conclusion

6 Better equipment is not always a bad thing, of course. New equipment can certainly be good for a sport. For example, tennis racquets used to be wooden. The heavy rackets could break and cause injuries. In the 1980s, companies introduced new high-tech carbon racquets, which are easier and safer to use. The new racquets have made tennis more enjoyable for the average tennis player. Technology has improved equipment in all sports, from downhill skiing to bicycle racing.

agree

7 The question is this: When does technology create an unfair advantage? In the future, sports engineers may invent an artificial leg that is better than a real leg. Will it be acceptable for competitions? Do high-tech contact lenses give golfers an advantage? Can runners use special shoes that help them run faster while using less **energy**? These questions do not have easy answers. We must make sure that technology does not make sports unfair. However, we should welcome improvements that make sports more enjoyable and safer for all.

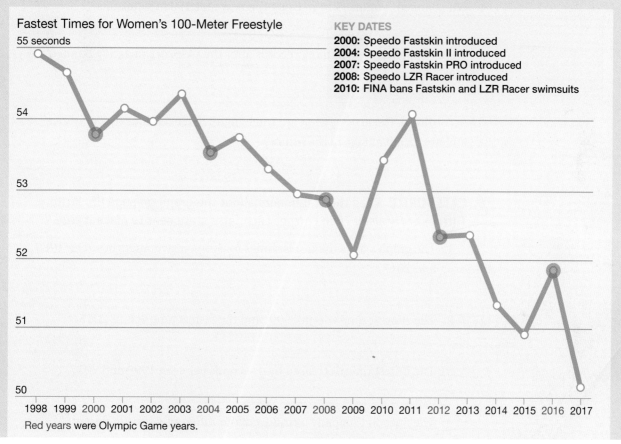

Fastest Times for Women's 100-Meter Freestyle

KEY DATES
2000: Speedo Fastskin introduced
2004: Speedo Fastskin II introduced
2007: Speedo Fastskin PRO introduced
2008: Speedo LZR Racer introduced
2010: FINA bans Fastskin and LZR Racer swimsuits

Red years were Olympic Game years.

B. IDENTIFY Read one student's notes for the article. Write the correct paragraph number next to each note to show the correct order.

✓ 6 a. Some improvements are good; sports become easier, safer.

✓ 4 b. Swimmers broke many new records in 2008–2009; FINA banned suits in 2010.

✓ 1 c. Athletes always look for ways to improve performance.

✓ 5 d. After ban, swimmers broke few records.

✓ 3 e. Engineers invented new material; like shark skin.

✓ 2 f. Technology can give athletes an advantage.

✓ 7 g. Many questions about technology and sports; no easy answers.

C. IDENTIFY Answer these questions.

1. Why are some people concerned about technology in sports?

_____

2. What were the advantages of the full-body swimsuits?

_____

3. How did people know that the new swimsuit material gave swimmers an advantage?

_____

4. Who banned swimmers from using the new material in swimsuits?

_____

5. What happened to swimming records after the swim organization banned the suits?

_____

6. According to the article, what are some high-tech inventions that may give athletes an advantage in the future?

_____

D. CATEGORIZE Read the statements about the graph on page 85. Write T (true) or F (false). Then correct each false statement to make it true.

_____ 1. The graph shows the fastest times for women swimmers between 1989 and 2017.

_____

_____ 2. The slowest time was in 1999, and the fastest time was in 2015.

_____

_____ 3. The fastest time decreased by 4 seconds between 1999 and 2017.

_____

_____ 4. The Speedo Company introduced four different swimsuit designs between 2000 and 2008.

_____

_____ 5. Overall, times have increased between 2012 and 2017.

_____

E. DISCUSS Discuss these questions with a partner or a group.

1. Some swimmers were in favor of the new swimsuit material. List three reasons swimmers might be in favor of the material.

2. Even though the swimsuit material was banned in 2010, times continued to drop. Why do you think swimmers kept swimming faster?

WORK WITH THE VIDEO

A. PREVIEW What do you do if you get lost? Do you ask a stranger for directions, use a map, or use your phone? Which method do you think is most helpful?

VIDEO VOCABULARY

pinpoint (v.) to find the exact position of something

orbit (v.) to move around something

receiver (n.) a piece of radio or television equipment that changes broadcast signals into sound or pictures

signal (n.) a series of electrical waves that carry sounds, pictures, or messages, for example, to a radio, television, or cell phone

calculate (v.) to find something out by using mathematics

iQ RESOURCES Go online to watch the video about how GPS works.
Resources > Video > Unit 4 > Unit Video

B. CATEGORIZE Watch the video two or three times. Write *T* (true) or *F* (false) for each statement. Correct the false statements.

1 GPS means Global Positioning System. ____

2. GPS uses satellites that orbit the moon. ____

3. There are always at least six satellites for a GPS device to access. ____

4. GPS works by calculating the distance between the receiver and a satellite. ____

5. It uses the speed of the signal and the time it takes to travel from the Earth to the receiver. ____

6. In total, two satellites are needed to pinpoint the location of the GPS device. ____

7. GPS is used to manage transport systems and military operations, but it is most often used by individuals to find locations such as the nearest cafe! ____

C. DISCUSS Discuss the questions with a group.

1. Do you think GPS makes people lazy or improves their knowledge of their surroundings?

2. In what specific situations could GPS make companies or organizations improve their performance? For example, in what situations could it save money or improve customer service?

WRITE WHAT YOU THINK

SYNTHESIZE Think about Reading 1, Reading 2, and the unit video as you discuss these questions. Then choose one question and write a response.

1. In the Olympic Games, competitions should be fair. Do you think they are? What can make a competition unfair at the Olympics?

2. In addition to money and technology, what else can improve an athlete's performance? In your opinion, what can make the biggest difference?

VOCABULARY SKILL Using the dictionary

Understanding additional information

A dictionary gives you more than just the definition of a word. It also gives you other useful information. For example:

- the pronunciation of the word
- the part of speech
- example sentences to show how to use the word correctly
- other forms of the word

When you read the example sentences, notice which prepositions are used with a particular verb. Notice which nouns are used with a particular adjective. Understanding additional information in a dictionary will help you learn how to use new words correctly.

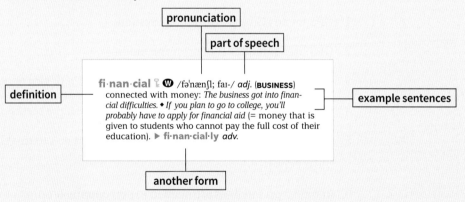

All dictionary entries adapted from the *Oxford American Dictionary for learners of English* © Oxford University Press 2011.

A. APPLY Read the dictionary entry below. Then answer the questions.

> **com·pete** 🔉 ⓦ /kəmˈpit/ *verb* [I] **compete (against/with sb) (for sth)** to try to win or achieve something, or to try to be better than someone else: *The world's best athletes compete in the Olympic Games.* ♦ *The teams are competing for the state championship.* ♦ *When they were kids, they always used to compete with each other.* ♦ *They had to compete against several larger companies to get the contract.*

1. Which prepositions are used with the verb **compete**? _____

2. Which prepositions are used in these phrases?

   a. compete _____ or _____ a person

   b. compete _____ the championship

   c. compete _____ each other

   d. compete _____ the Olympic Games

3. Which example sentence shows that *compete* is not just for sports?

   _____

4. Using the example sentences as a guide, write two of your own sentences with *compete*.

   _____

   _____

TIP FOR SUCCESS

Be sure you know the abbreviations and meanings for parts of speech in a dictionary.

n. noun

v. verb

adj. adjective

adv. adverb

prep. preposition

conj. conjunction

B. IDENTIFY Use your dictionary to answer the questions.

1. What part of speech is the word *responsibility*? *responsible*?

   _____ , _____

2. The word *expert* is a noun. What other part of speech can it be?

   _____

3. What parts of speech is the word *profit*? *profitable*?

   _____ and _____ , _____

4. What is the plural form of *ability*? _____

iQ PRACTICE Go online for more practice with using the dictionary.
Practice ⟩ Unit 4 ⟩ Activity 8

WRITING

OBJECTIVE ▶ At the end of this unit, you will write an opinion paragraph about using technology to improve performance in sports or in education. This paragraph will include specific information from the readings and your own ideas.

WRITING SKILL Writing an opinion paragraph

In an opinion paragraph, you give your ideas about a topic. Writers often introduce their opinions with these phrases:

I (do not) think (that); I (do not) believe (that); In my opinion; I feel (that)

> I do not think that using technology can make you a better runner.
>
> I believe that runners spend too much time looking at data from their fitness watches.

WRITING TIP

Phrases that introduce your opinions (*I believe that, I think that*) can make your opinions sound more polite.

In an opinion paragraph, you want to make the reader agree with your opinion, so you need to support your opinion with reasons and supporting details or examples.

> Fitness watches can be addictive, so runners look at them all of the time.
>
> Second, fitness watches only show your time and your heart rate.
>
> Third, if you focus on enjoying your run, your times will naturally improve.

Your paragraph should end with a strong concluding sentence. Your concluding sentence should restate the topic of your paragraph and your opinion about it.

> For these reasons, I believe that runners depend too much on technology.
>
> I feel strongly that listening to your own body as you run will result in better times.

A. WRITING MODEL Read the model opinion paragraph. Then answer the questions on page 91.

As technology becomes more and more advanced, athletes will soon have contact lenses that do more than correct vision problems. High-tech contact lenses can greatly improve eyesight so that an athlete's eyesight is much stronger than the average person's. This gives an unfair advantage to some athletes. In my opinion, sports organizations ought to have rules against contact lenses in competitions. Eyesight is extremely important in sports like golf and baseball. Athletes have to see objects that are very far away. For this reason, if they have super-vision because of high-tech contact lenses, they will play better than other athletes. We already have reports that this is true. Professional golfers say that high-tech contact lenses have greatly improved their performance. The cost is another reason I am against high-tech contact lenses. These lenses are too expensive for many players. Players who cannot afford them are at a disadvantage. For these reasons, I feel strongly that there must be rules against high-tech contact lenses in some sports.

1. In which sentence does the writer introduce the opinion? What phrase signals the opinion?

    _____

2. Where does the writer give background information about the topic?

    _____

3. What are the two reasons for the writer's opinion?

    _____

4. What phrase signals each reason?

    _____

5. Where does the writer restate the paragraph topic?

    _____

B. IDENTIFY Fill in the graphic organizer with information from the paragraph on page 90.

Opinion

Sports organizations ought to have _____.

Reason

They can give athletes _____.

Reason

_____ are very expensive.

Supporting details

Eyesight is extremely important

Supporting details

CRITICAL THINKING STRATEGY

Organizing ideas with a graphic organizer

To **organize ideas**, it is helpful to use a graphic organizer. It will help you plan your writing. For example, a graphic organizer can help you see the overall structure, distinguish between parts, and categorize ideas. Your graphic organizer will change depending on your topic and how you will present your ideas.

You can also use a graphic organizer to analyze and take notes on a text you are reading. This is what you did in Activity B on page 91.

iQ PRACTICE   Go online to watch the Critical Thinking Video and check your comprehension. *Practice > Unit 4 > Activity 9*

C. EXTEND Choose a topic for an opinion paragraph. Then plan your writing. Make a graphic organizer similar to the one in Activity B. Fill it in with ideas for your paragraph. Include reasons, supporting details, and examples.

Topic A: What sport do you think is the best for a young child to learn?

Topic B: Some parents encourage students to specialize in just one sport at a very early age. They want their children to be very skilled and competitive. Is this a good idea?

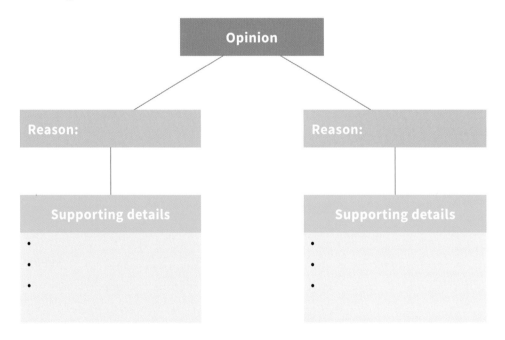

D. COMPOSE Write sentences to use in your paragraph.

1. Write a sentence introducing your opinion. Remember, this is usually not the first sentence in the paragraph.

_____

2. Write a concluding sentence. It can restate your opinion in different words.

_____

E. COMPOSE Write an opinion paragraph. Use your graphic organizer from Activity C and your sentences from Activity D.

iQ PRACTICE Go online for more practice with opinion paragraphs.
Practice › Unit 4 › Activity 10

GRAMMAR Modals

One way to give your opinion is to use the **modals** *should, should (not),* and *ought to.*

> Professional athletes **should** use the latest sports technology.
> Coaches **ought to follow** the rules.
> I believe that new high-tech materials **should be** approved by sports organizations.

Note that *ought not* is rarely used.

To make a very strong statement of your opinion, you can use *must* and *must not*.

> Officials **must keep** a close eye on athletes' equipment.
> We **must not let** sports be unfair in our schools.

A. IDENTIFY Look at the paragraph on page 90. Circle the modals *ought to* and *must*.

B. APPLY Complete the first part of these sentences using *should, should not,* or *ought to*. Then finish the sentence with your own ideas. Use each modal at least once. Then compare and discuss your answers with a partner.

1. I think medical schools _____ use virtual reality to train medical students because _____.

2. I believe that universities _____ use virtual reality in all of their programs because _____.

3. In my opinion, athletes _____ become familiar with new technology because _____.

4. I believe that sports organizations such as the Olympic Games _____ evaluate all improvements to equipment because _____.

C. IDENTIFY Look back at your opinion paragraph in Activity E on page 93. Underline the modals. If there are no modals, rewrite some of your sentences to include modals.

iQ PRACTICE Go online for more practice with modals.
Practice > Unit 4 > Activities 11–12

UNIT ASSIGNMENT Write an opinion paragraph

OBJECTIVE ▶

In this assignment, you will write an opinion paragraph. As you prepare your paragraph, think about the Unit Question, "How can technology improve performance?" Use information from Reading 1, Reading 2, the unit video, and your work in this unit to support your opinion paragraph. Refer to the Self-Assessment checklist on page 96.

---

iQ PRACTICE Go online to the Writing Tutor to read a model opinion paragraph. *Practice > Unit 4 > Activity 13*

PLAN AND WRITE

A. BRAINSTORM Complete the activities.

1. When can technology improve performance in education or in sports? Should this technology be used more? Brainstorm a list of ideas.

_____

_____

_____

2. Circle two or three of the best ideas on your list.

B. PLAN Discuss your ideas from Activity A in a group. Then write your opinions as a topic sentence for your paragraph and complete the graphic organizer with your reasons and supporting details.

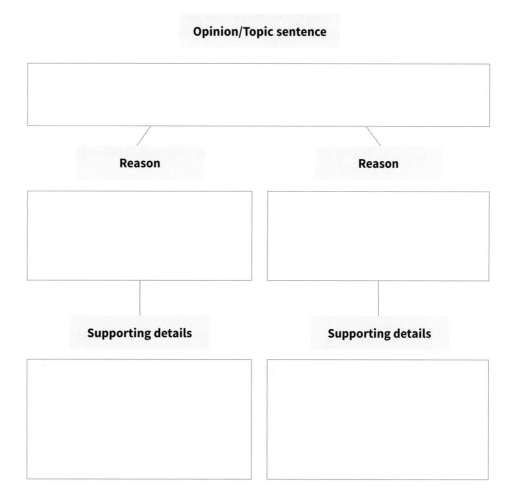

Opinion/Topic sentence

Reason

Reason

Supporting details

Supporting details

iQ RESOURCES Go online to download and complete the outline for your opinion paragraph. _Resources > Writing Tools > Unit 4 > Outline_

WRITING TIP

Remember to begin your paragraph with some background information about the topic. Then introduce your opinion. See how the writer did this in the opinion paragraph in Activity A, on page 90.

C. WRITE Use your planning notes to write your opinion paragraph.

1. Include phrases from the Writing Skill on page 90 to introduce your opinions. Use the modals *should* (*not*), *ought to*, and *must* (*not*) to give your opinion. Be sure that your paragraph ends with a strong concluding sentence.

2. Look at the Self-Assessment checklist to guide your writing.

iQ PRACTICE Go online to the Writing Tutor to write your assignment.
Practice > Unit 4 > Activity 14

REVISE AND EDIT

iQ RESOURCES Go online to download the peer review worksheet.
Resources > Writing Tools > Unit 4 > Peer Review Worksheet

A. PEER REVIEW Read your partner's paragraph. Then use the peer review worksheet. Discuss the review with your partner.

B. REWRITE Based on your partner's review, revise and rewrite your opinion paragraph.

C. EDIT Complete the Self-Assessment checklist as you prepare to write the final draft of your opinion paragraph. Be prepared to hand in your work or discuss it in class.

SELF-ASSESSMENT	Yes	No
Do you support your opinion with reasons, supporting details, and examples?	☐	☐
Underline any modals in your paragraph. Do you use the base form of verbs after modals?	☐	☐
Is each word used correctly? Check a dictionary if you are not sure.	☐	☐
Does the opinion paragraph include vocabulary from the unit?	☐	☐
Did you check the paragraph for punctuation, spelling, and grammar?	☐	☐

D. REFLECT Discuss these questions with a partner or group.

1. What is something new you learned in this unit?

2. Look back at the Unit Question—How can technology improve performance? Is your answer different now than when you started the unit? If yes, how is it different? Why?

iQ PRACTICE Go to the online discussion board to discuss the questions.
Practice > Unit 4 > Activity 15

TRACK YOUR SUCCESS

iQ PRACTICE Go online to check the words and phrases you have learned in this unit. *Practice > Unit 4 > Activity 16*

Check (✓) the skills you learned. If you need more work on a skill, refer to the page(s) in parentheses.

READING	☐ I can take notes. (p. 81)
VOCABULARY	☐ I can use the dictionary to learn additional information about a word. (p. 88)
WRITING	☐ I can write an opinion paragraph. (p. 90)
CRITICAL THINKING	☐ I can organize ideas using a graphic organizer. (p. 92)
GRAMMAR	☐ I can use modals correctly. (p. 93)

OBJECTIVE ▶ ☐ I can gather information and ideas to write an opinion paragraph about how to improve performance with technology.

Business

What makes a family business successful?

A. Discuss these questions with your classmates.

1. Do you know anyone who owns a family business? What kind of business is it? Do you think it is successful?

2. Look at the photo. Who are the people? What can make this type of business successful?

B. Listen to *The Q Classroom* online. Then answer these questions.

1. According to Sophy, why is her uncle's business successful?

2. Do you think family members are better employees? Why or why not?

iQ PRACTICE Go to the online discussion board to discuss the Unit Question with your classmates. *Practice > Unit 5 > Activity 1*

UNIT OBJECTIVE

Read the articles. Gather information and ideas to write a plan for a successful family business.

READING 1

A Successful Family Business

You are going to read a magazine article about a successful family business. Use the article to gather information and ideas for your Unit Assignment.

PREVIEW THE READING

TIP FOR SUCCESS

When you read a new word, remember to use the context of the sentence to help you figure out the meaning.

A. VOCABULARY Here are some words from Reading 1. Read their definitions. Then complete each sentence.

> **corporation** *(noun)* a big company
>
> **courage** *(noun)* 🔑 the ability to control your fear when you do something dangerous or difficult
>
> **design** *(verb)* 🔑 OPAL to plan and develop how something will look
>
> **expand** *(verb)* 🔑 OPAL to become bigger or make something become bigger
>
> **expert** *(noun)* 🔑 OPAL a person who knows a lot about something
>
> **manage** *(verb)* 🔑 to control someone or something
>
> **strength** *(noun)* 🔑 OPAL a good quality or ability that someone or something has
>
> **unity** *(noun)* a situation in which people are working together or in agreement

🔑 Oxford 3000™ words   OPAL Oxford Phrasal Academic Lexicon

1. Nawaf and Mohanad showed a lot of _____ when they left their country to open a business in France.

2. We hired an architect to help us _____ our new home.

3. Mr. Gibbs is a(n) _____ on restaurant management. He has managed restaurants for 20 years and has written a book on the subject.

4. The Smiths have a strong sense of _____ in their family. They always take care of each other.

5. Our business only has six employees now, but we think it will _____ a lot over the next few years.

6. Turki's greatest _____ is his ability to keep a positive attitude when times are difficult.

7. Ford, a car company, is an extremely large _____.

8. Mr. Al Jaser is a great teacher. I don't know how he can _____ all of those children.

iQ PRACTICE Go online for more practice with the vocabulary.
Practice > Unit 5 > Activities 2–3

B. PREVIEW Look at the images in Reading 1. What kind of business do you think the article is about? Use the chart below to think of some advantages and disadvantages of working with family members in a business.

Advantages	Disadvantages

WRITING TIP
When you are writing, try to think of other points of view. Write your own idea, but also think about what someone else might think. Try to use some other ideas as well.

C. QUICK WRITE Would you open a family business? Write a short paragraph to answer the question. Use your chart from Activity B to describe the advantages and disadvantages of working in a family business. Be sure to use this section for your Unit Assignment.

READING SKILL Skimming

Skimming is reading a text quickly to get the general idea of what it is about. Skimming is useful when you read a newspaper or magazine, read online, or take a test. When you do research, you skim an article to see if it will be useful. When you skim, use these tips.

- Read the title.
- Look at any images and read any captions.
- Quickly read the first sentence of each paragraph.
- Move your eyes quickly through the text.
- Do not read every sentence or every word.
- If the text is short, read the first and last sentence of each paragraph.

A. IDENTIFY Take one minute to skim Reading 1 on pages 102–103. As you skim, underline the first sentence of each paragraph.

B. RESTATE Write what you can remember about the reading.

C. CATEGORIZE Take one minute to skim Reading 2 on pages 107–108. Then compare the contents of Reading 1 and Reading 2.

Which reading has information about . . .	Reading 1	Reading 2
1. a family that owned a newspaper	☐	☑
2. an industrial business	☐	☐
3. family businesses in the United States	☐	☐
4. a company that delivers products and services	☐	☐
5. difficulties with family businesses	☐	☐

iQ PRACTICE Go online for more practice with skimming.
Practice > Unit 5 > Activity 4

WORK WITH THE READING

A. INVESTIGATE Read the magazine article and gather information about what makes a family business successful.

A SUCCESSFUL **FAMILY BUSINESS**

1 It started with the **courage** of a young man, Abdullah Al Hamad Al Zamil. Born in the small farming town of Onaiza, Saudi Arabia, Al Zamil was determined to start his own business. To do this, he moved from Saudi Arabia to Bahrain and began a trading business. It was 1926, and he was only 19 years old. At first, he traded mostly food items and textiles such as material for clothing and bedding. In the 1930s, he started his company. Soon, he decided to **expand** his business to include real estate: the buying and selling of land and buildings. He was a very successful businessperson, and his company grew quickly. Al Zamil expanded his business into other areas as well and built what was then one of the tallest buildings in Al Khobar, Saudi Arabia.

2 Al Zamil had a large family, and his 12 sons were always an important part of the family business. After his death in 1961, the sons continued to work together to keep the Zamil Group going. They wanted the business to continue to grow in the spirit of their hardworking father, so they expanded into new areas. First, they invested in making parts for machines, and later they added the manufacturing of steel and glass. They worked to **design** new products and became **experts** in new technology.

3   While running the company, Al Zamil's sons always remember what their parents taught them: to be modest[1], honest, hardworking, and respectful of older generations[2]. The family makes decisions by consensus—that is, by making sure that everyone agrees before moving ahead. This practice helps keep a feeling of **unity**. Finally, demonstrating the sharp business sense[3] that they share with their father, Al Zamil's sons understand the value of taking risks from time to time. This, along with the **strength** in their close family relationship, has been a key to their success.

4   Today, what began as a small family business over 85 years ago is now a huge **corporation**. The Zamil Group has more than 12,000 workers in over 60 countries. It also owns many different companies. They **manage** construction, shipbuilding, plastic, chemical, and paint companies. They have bought some smaller companies and also work as a partner with other companies in India, Germany, and the United States. Their goal is to deliver high-quality products and services around the world.

5   It is difficult for a family business to remain strong over the years. The Zamils keep their company strong by separating[4] the owners from the managers and by being very professional. "It is necessary that the second and third generations prove their . . . skills to do the job properly," says Khalid A. Al Zamil. The next generation shouldn't have high positions just because they are sons of the owners, he adds. Clearly, the success of the Zamil Group is thanks to the strong leadership of the family members, combined with strong family values.

---

[1] **modest:** not talking much about good things you have done
[2] **generation:** all the people in a family who were born around the same time
[3] **sharp business sense:** ability to do well in business
[4] **separating:** dividing

B. IDENTIFY Circle the answer to each question.

1. What is the main idea of paragraph 3?

   a. The sons expanded the business into new areas.

   b. There is strength in family unity.

   c. Only family businesses are successful.

2. What is the main idea of paragraph 4?

   a. The business became a large corporation.

   b. The group has many manufacturing locations.

   c. One branch of the company focuses on steel and chemical products.

3. What is the main idea of the entire article?

   a. Any family can become a big success.

   b. Family members have different strengths.

   c. A family that works together can be successful.

C. IDENTIFY Write the correct paragraph number next to each detail.

____ a. Their father taught them to be hardworking.

____ b. The younger generation needs to prove their skills.

____ c. The Zamil Group has more than 12,000 employees.

____ d. Al Zamil built one of the tallest buildings in Saudi Arabia.

____ e. The brothers became experts in new technology.

D. IDENTIFY Complete the paragraphs below with details from the reading.

In 1926, Abdullah Al Hamad Al Zamil moved to Bahrain. There he began

a _____ business. At first, he traded mostly
      1

_____ items and _____ .
            2   3

Before long he decided to _____ his business, and he
                                          4

became very _____ . Later on, his sons operated the
                      5

business. They _____ in industrial manufacturing
                        6

and worked to _____ new products. Their
                        7

father taught them to be modest, honest, _____ ,
                                                      8

and respectful. He also taught them that it was a good idea to take

_____ . Today the Zamil Group is a large
          9

_____ that owns many different companies.
          10

E. IDENTIFY Answer these questions.

1. How old was Abdullah Zamil when he moved to Bahrain?

_____

2. What contributed to the Zamil family's success?

_____

3. What ideas did Abdullah Al Zamil share with his children?

_____

4. Why do you think the Zamil Group decided to work together with companies in other countries?

_____

5. Are the family owners also the managers of the business? Why or why not?

_____

F. IDENTIFY Number these events in the order in which they occurred.

____ a. Al Zamil expanded his business to include real estate.

____ b. The business expanded into industrial manufacturing.

____ c. The company worked to separate the family owners from the company management.

____ d. Al Zamil traded food items and textiles.

____ e. Abdullah Al Zamil began his trading business in Bahrain.

____ f. The Zamil Group began working with companies in other countries.

____ g. After the death of Al Zamil, his sons kept the business going.

____ h. The family business became a huge corporation.

iQ PRACTICE Go online for additional reading and comprehension.
Practice > Unit 5 > Activity 5

? WRITE WHAT YOU THINK

A. DISCUSS Ask and answer these questions with a partner.

1. What strengths did the Zamil family have? How did these help them have a successful business?

2. What strengths do you have that help you when working in a group?

B. COMPOSE Choose one of the questions from Activity A and write a response. Use supporting examples. Look back at your Quick Write on page 101 as you think about what you learned.

Question: _____

My Response: _____

_____

_____

READING 2

The Challenge of Running a Family Business

OBJECTIVE ▶

You are going to read a textbook article about the difficulties of owning a family business. Use the article to gather information and ideas for your Unit Assignment.

PREVIEW THE READING

VOCABULARY SKILL REVIEW

In Unit 4, you used the dictionary to learn about pronunciation, parts of speech, and related forms of words. Use your dictionary to check on the pronunciation and related word forms of *challenge, enthusiasm, realistic,* and *responsibility.*

A. VOCABULARY Here are some words from Reading 2. Read the sentences. Circle the answer that best matches the meaning of each <u>underlined</u> word or phrase.

1. For many parents, communicating with their teenage children can be a big <u>challenge</u>. At this age, children may not want to talk to their parents about <u>their problems.</u>

   a. an exciting event

   b. a difficult thing that makes you try hard

2. Thamer will be a great sports reporter because of his great <u>enthusiasm</u> for sports.

   a. difficulty with something

   b. strong feeling of liking something

3. My children <u>depend on</u> me to drive them to school.

   a. need someone to provide something

   b. help someone

4. Ali's store isn't <u>making much money</u>. He's worried that it's going to <u>fail</u>.

   a. be unsuccessful

   b. break the law

5. Ahmed's <u>goal</u> for <u>the future</u> is to join the family business.

   a. thing that you want to do

   b. subject that you study

6. Fatimah is <u>spending more time</u> with her friends and <u>less time studying</u>. Her father is worried about her change in <u>lifestyle</u>.

   a. the way that you dress

   b. the way that you live

7. My grandmother will <u>pass down</u> her jewelry to my mother.

   a. give something to a younger person

   b. create something

8. Jack still thinks he's going to become a basketball star. He needs to be more <u>realistic</u> about his career.

    a. interested and excited

    b. understanding what is possible

9. Carl's <u>responsibility</u> at home is taking out the garbage. His brother has to set the table for dinner.

    a. things that you must buy

    b. jobs or duties that you must do

10. My cousin has a <u>talent</u> for writing. She writes wonderful stories.

    a. natural skill or ability

    b. thing you want

iQ PRACTICE Go online for more practice with the vocabulary. *Practice > Unit 5 > Activities 6–7*

TIP FOR SUCCESS
When you are skimming a text, use a pencil tip to help your eyes move quickly across the text, or place a piece of paper under each line as your read. This will help you avoid stopping to read every word.

B. PREVIEW Skim the reading. Which paragraph gives an example of an actual family business?

C. QUICK WRITE What problems might owners of a family business have? Write a few sentences before you read. Be sure to use this section for your Unit Assignment.

WORK WITH THE READING

A. INVESTIGATE Read the article about the challenges of running a family business and gather information about what makes a family business successful.

The Challenge of Running a Family Business

1   In the United States, families own about 85 percent of all businesses. However, less than 30 percent of these companies last more than 20 years. The companies **fail**, and the owners can't **pass down** the family businesses to their sons and daughters. Why is it so difficult for family businesses to survive?

The Wall Street Journal

give something

2   One reason may be changing times. Fifty years ago, many families owned local grocery stores. But today, small family-owned stores cannot compete with large supermarket chains. Today, most Mom and Pop stores[1] are a thing of the past[2]. The way of life is another **challenge** in a family business. A successful company requires hard work and long hours. Younger generations may not want this **lifestyle**. They may want more freedom. In addition, sons and daughters may not have the same **enthusiasm** for the business as their parents.

3   A successful family business **depends on** the family's strengths and **talents**. However, families also bring their weaknesses and personal problems to the workplace. Many families do not communicate well, and they are not good at solving problems together. These challenges often cause businesses to fail. According to Professor Randel Carlock, these problems are common. He says, "Being part of a family is very difficult. Being part of a family business is even more difficult." Love is important in a family, but love is not enough to run a family business. The business must achieve financial success.

4   The Bancroft family is an interesting example. For 105 years, the Bancroft family owned *The Wall Street Journal*. It is one of the most famous newspapers in the United States. But there were many family problems. They did not communicate well, and they disagreed about many things. One person said that they couldn't even agree on where to go for lunch! The younger family members wanted the business to be more profitable. The older members thought the quality of the paper was more important than making money. In addition, the family let people outside of the family manage the newspaper. They did not take part in many important decisions. Finally, in 2007, all 33 of the Bancroft family owners agreed to sell the company. Although the business had lasted several generations, the Bancrofts eventually had to sell their company because they did not manage it well. In the end, many of their family relationships suffered.

5   Many families dream of passing down their businesses to the next generation, but this requires careful planning and preparation. Good management is a key to success. All employees, especially family members, need to have clear **responsibilities**. Family business owners need to think about how decisions are made. Also, they should be **realistic** about the dreams and **goals** of the younger generation. Family businesses can be successful because of strong family ties[3]. But to succeed for more than one generation, families need to manage their businesses carefully.

Less than 30 percent of family businesses last more than 20 years.

[1] **Mom and Pop stores:** stores owned by a family or individual, not a corporation
[2] **thing of the past:** something that no longer exists
[3] **ties:** something that connects you with other people

by Tuesday

B. CATEGORIZE Read the statements. Write *T* (true) or *F* (false). Then correct each false statement to make it true. Write the paragraph number where the answer is found.

~~X~~ 50 1. Fifty percent of family businesses are passed down to the next generation.

Paragraph: 1 *In U.S, familys own about 85% of all businesses*
However   less tan 30% of these companies last

Q 2. Most family businesses cannot compete with big companies.

Paragraph: 2 _____

Q 3. A lot of family businesses want to pass down the businesses to their sons and daughters.

Paragraph: 5 _____

X 4. The Bancroft family managed their newspaper by themselves.

Paragraph: 4 *The Bancrofts eventually had to sell*
their company

C. IDENTIFY Look back at paragraph 1 in Reading 2 to find the missing information for the sentences below.

1. In the United States, families own about _85_ percent of all businesses. However, less than _30_ percent of these businesses last more than _20_ years.

2. Write each phrase from the box in the correct section of the pie charts.

① Family-owned businesses
② Family-owned businesses that last more than 20 years
③ Family-owned businesses that fail within 20 years
④ Businesses that are not family-owned

④ ✓ _____   _____ 3 ✓
15%   70%
① ✓ _____   _____ ②
      85%   30%

D. EXPLAIN Look back at Reading 2 on pages 107–108 to find reasons why family businesses fail. Write two of the reasons below. Then compare your answers with a partner.

_____

_____

WORK WITH THE VIDEO

A. PREVIEW Do you like eating candy or chocolate? What are your favorite kinds?

VIDEO VOCABULARY

expand (v.) to become bigger or to make something bigger

manage (v.) to be in charge or control of something

smooth (adj.) [of a liquid] without lumps

flavor (n.) the taste and smell of food

iQ RESOURCES Go online to watch the video about a small family business that became a large company. *Resources > Video > Unit 5 > Unit Video*

B. APPLY Watch the video two or three times. Complete the sentences with the words in the box.

Zurich	father	170	son	machine
factory	chocolate-maker	biggest	quality	

1. The Lindt company has been in business for more than _____ years.

2. It was started by a _____ and _____.

3. Their first chocolate shop was in _____.

4. As well as selling chocolate, they decided to build a _____.

5. Johann went into business with a _____ called Rodolphe Lindt.

6. The chocolate was so delicious because they used a special _____.

7. The _____ of their products is an important reason for their success.

8. They are now one of the _____ candy companies in the world.

C. DISCUSS Discuss the questions with a group.

1. What were some reasons that the Lindt chocolate company became successful?

2. What advantages do you think family businesses have over other businesses?

3. What might be some difficulties in helping a company grow internationally?

WRITE WHAT YOU THINK

SYNTHESIZE Think about Reading 1, Reading 2, and the unit video as you discuss these questions. Then choose one question and write a response.

1. What are some advantages to working in the same business with your family? What are some disadvantages?

2. Why do you think most small businesses fail in the first few years?

 CRITICAL THINKING STRATEGY

Drawing conclusions

When you draw conclusions, you combine ideas from several sources to form an opinion or make a decision about a topic. You may change your opinion or think of new ideas about the topic. A good way to start is by summarizing the ideas from the sources. Look at these student notes.

Source	Ideas
Newspaper	For the best jobs, the top five college majors are: computer science, communications, political science, business, and economics.
TV news video	The six most popular college majors are: business, health, social sciences, history, biomedical sciences, and engineering.
Personal experience	My cousin tells me that there are many good jobs available in biomedical sciences. His friends who major in business or economics are having a hard time finding jobs. My teachers tell me that there are many jobs for computer science majors.

Next, you synthesize the ideas to draw your conclusion. That is, you bring them together and see what new ideas you have about the topic. The last two sentences are your conclusion.

There are many different opinions about the best college major. A recent newspaper article listed the top college majors for getting a good job. These included computer science, communications, and business. On the other hand, a recent TV news video said that business, biomedical sciences, and engineering were some of the most popular college majors. My teachers and friends all give me different opinions about the best college major. For me, I think I need to choose an area of study that interests me, that I am good at, and that will help me find a job. I used to think that a business major would be the best, but now I am thinking about computer science.

iQ PRACTICE Go online to watch the Critical Thinking Video and check your comprehension. *Practice › Unit 5 › Activity 8*

A. IDENTIFY Read the question. Use phrases from the box to fill in the chart to summarize ideas from Reading 1, Reading 2, and the unit video. Then add your own ideas.

What are the keys to making a family business successful?

be realistic about goals	have good management
develop new products	have strong family values
have clear responsibilities	separate the owners from the managers
have courage to expand the business	be careful about quality

Source	
Reading 1	
Reading 2	
Unit video	
Own ideas	

B. SYNTHESIZE Synthesize your ideas to draw conclusions about what makes a family business successful. Write a paragraph of at least four sentences. Summarize what you have learned in the unit and then add your own thoughts.

What are the keys to making a family business successful?

_____

_____

_____

_____

C. SYNTHESIZE Think about Reading 1, Reading 2, and the unit video as you discuss these questions. Then choose one question and write a response. Write four sentences.

1. What differences do you see in the three family businesses: Lindt and Sprüngli (chocolate), the Zamils (trade, manufacturing, investment), and the Bancrofts (newspaper)?

2. Why do you think that the Zamil family was successful but the Bancroft family had to sell their business?

Understanding grammatical information in the dictionary

When you look up a word in the dictionary, pay attention to the grammatical information. In addition to the part of speech, an entry may also tell you:

- if a noun is countable (C) or uncountable (U)
- if the plural of a noun has an irregular form
- if an adjective or adverb has an irregular comparative form
- if a verb has an irregular form

Looking up and understanding grammatical information about a new word helps you use the word correctly.

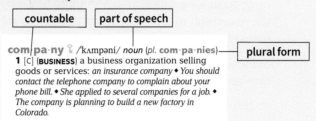

All dictionary entries adapted from the *Oxford American Dictionary for learners of English* © Oxford University Press 2011.

A. IDENTIFY Use your dictionary to answer these questions.

1. Which words are uncountable? Circle them.

advantage	happiness	participant
advice	information	planet
darkness	luggage	police
furniture	news	traffic

ACADEMIC LANGUAGE

The noun *analysis* is commonly used in academic articles.
The analysis of the data was done by computer.

_____ OPAL
Oxford Phrasal Academic Lexicon

2. What is the plural form of each of these nouns?

   a. analysis _____   c. child _____

   b. cactus _____   d. life _____

3. What is the simple past form of each of these phrases?

   a. break down _____

   b. burst into _____

   c. shine at _____

iQ PRACTICE Go online for more practice with using the dictionary.
Practice > Unit 5 > Activity 9

WRITING

OBJECTIVE ▶

For this unit, you will gather information and ideas to write a plan for a successful family business. This plan will include specific information from the readings and your own ideas.

WRITING SKILL Unity in a paragraph

A paragraph is a group of sentences about a single idea. The topic sentence introduces the audience to the topic. The concluding sentence may summarize the contents of the paragraph. The sentences in the middle provide details to support the main idea. All of the sentences in the paragraph should be about the same main idea. The sentences should be closely related to each other. This gives the paragraph **unity**—all parts of the paragraph work together to support a single main idea.

Sentences or ideas that are <u>not</u> closely related to the main idea are irrelevant—they do not help explain and support the main idea.

To be relevant, your sentences should:

- be <u>directly</u> related to the main idea
- support the main idea, but not repeat it
- give new information or details that support the main idea
- not introduce an entirely new main idea that is different from the topic sentence

When you edit your writing, remove or change any sentences that are irrelevant. If all the sentences clearly contribute to the main idea, your paragraph will have unity.

Transition words also keep your paragraphs unified. Transition words help your paragraphs read smoothly from one sentence to the next. They help the reader see the connections between ideas. Transition words can serve several purposes:

to add: *and, besides, finally, further, too, next, in addition, also, first (second, etc.)*

to give an example: *for example, for instance*

to emphasize: *definitely, obviously, always, certainly*

Use transition words to help keep your paragraphs unified.

iQ RESOURCES Go online to watch the Writing Skill Video.
Resources > Video > Unit 5 > Writing Skill Video

A. WRITING MODEL Read the model paragraph. Then answer the questions.

Many workers today have different options about how and where they work. Thanks to technology, some people can live far away from their offices and work from home. Computers and the Internet make it possible for individuals to telecommute—that is, to use the telephone and technology to get their work done without being in the office. In addition, since most computers now have microphones and video cameras, it is easy to have a meeting even when people are far away from each other. Now if someone gets a new job, they may not have to move to a new city. Maybe in the future, no one will work in an office at all. Everyone will work from home.

1. Circle the topic sentence that has the main idea.

2. How many supporting sentences are there? ____ Underline them.

3. Are all of the sentences in the paragraph about the same idea? _____

B. WRITING MODEL Read the model paragraph. Circle the main idea. Then cross out any unrelated sentences that don't help support the main idea.

People from the same family are sometimes quite different. Perhaps the father is usually quiet, while the mother is likely to be noisy. Brothers and sisters can also have very different personalities. Two brothers might both be very funny. There can also be large differences in appearance. Some family members may be tall, while others are short. Perhaps they have similar hair or faces. As you can see, family members may not be very similar at all.

C. APPLY Use the transition words from the box to complete the paragraph. For some sentences, there is more than one correct transition word.

finally	first	for instance	in addition	next

If you want to start a new school, there are several things you must consider. _____, you need to think about

what age group you will teach. _____ you
₂

must decide on the curriculum—the subject matter that you will teach.

_____, will your school teach driving, or will you
₃

teach photography? _____, you will need a place
₄

for students to study. _____ you need to decide how
₅

everyone will be paid.

D. WRITING MODEL Read the model paragraph describing a plan for a new business. Then answer the questions.

My business idea is to start a new math tutoring business. I am very good at math, and my classmates tell me that I explain things very clearly. I will tutor high school students in any math topic, including calculus. There are several reasons why I think my business will succeed. First, my business will be unique because all classes will be private. One-on-one attention will give students the chance to ask questions. In addition, all classes will be online. Obviously, online classes will be convenient for both the students and for me. We will use online video conferencing. Finally, each class will be only 20 minutes. Short classes will be easy to fit into any schedule. After class, the student will complete an assignment and turn it in to me for correction. I will advertise by putting up flyers at schools, libraries, and coffee shops. I hope to major in business when I attend college. I think my new business will be successful.

1. What is the main idea of the paragraph? _____

2. How many transition words do you see? _____ Circle them.

3. Do all of the ideas help support the main idea? _____

4. What are two questions you would like to ask the writer?

   _____

   _____

E. CREATE Brainstorm ideas about a plan for a special new school. What will the school be like? Who will the students be? What will you teach? It might be a school for language, photography, driving, or something else.

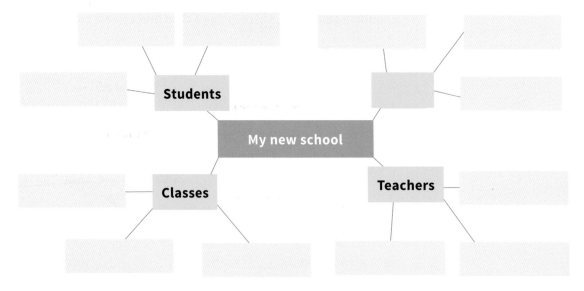

F. **COMPOSE** Write a paragraph describing a special new school. Use ideas from Activity E. Be sure you have a clear topic sentence and that all of the supporting ideas help unify the paragraph. Use transition words.

iQ PRACTICE Go online for more practice with paragraph unity.
Practice ⟩ Unit 5 ⟩ Activity 10

more | er | than   the most/est

GRAMMAR Comparative and superlative adjectives

Comparative adjectives describe the difference between two things.

For adjectives with one syllable, use *adjective + er*. *Than* often follows comparative adjectives.

tall	→	taller	The Burj Khalifa is **taller than** Taipei 101.
safe	→	safer	
big	→	bigger	

If an adjective ends in one vowel and one consonant, double the consonant.

big → bigger

If the adjective ends in *e*, just add *-r*.

safe → safer

For most adjectives with two or more syllables, use *more + adjective*.

| common | → | more common |
| traditional | → | more traditional |

For two-syllable adjectives that end in *-le*, add *-r*.

simple → simpler

For two-syllable adjectives that end in *-y*, change the *-y* to *i* and add *-er*.

pretty → prettier

Superlative adjectives describe three or more things.

For most adjectives that have one syllable, use *the + adjective + -est*.

tall	→	the tallest
big	→	the biggest
safe	→	the safest

For two-syllable adjectives that end in *-le*, use *the* and add *–st*.

simple → the simplest

For two-syllable adjectives that end in *-y*, change the *y* to *i*, use *the*, and add *-est*.

funny → the funniest

For most adjectives with two or more syllables, add *the + most + adjective*.

| informal | → | the most informal |
| realistic | → | the most realistic |

Note: Some adjectives are irregular.

| good | → | better | → | the best |
| bad | → | worse | → | the worst |

A. APPLY Complete the paragraph with words from the box. Change them into comparative form.

big	~~clear~~ *cr*	pretty *more*	realistic *more*	safe	~~simple~~ *more*

Many of us remember the good old days. Those times were

_____ *more simpler* _____ and less complicated. In those days, we felt
      1

much _____ *safer* _____ in our neighborhoods. There was less
       2

pollution, and the sky was _____ *clearer* _____. We may even
                            3

feel that nature was _____ *more pretty* _____ back then. As cities have
                      4

become _____ *bigger* _____, those days may be gone forever.
        5

Perhaps we all need to be _____ *more realistic* _____ about the future.
                           6

B. APPLY Complete each sentence with the correct comparative form of the adjective in parentheses.

1. I'm _____ *more successful* _____ (successful) in school than my brother is.

2. Hind is _____ *more rsbonsible* _____ (responsible) with her money than her younger
   sister is.

3. Elephants are _____ *more intelligent* _____ (intelligent) than fish.

4. People in small towns are often _____ *more friendly* _____ (friendly) than people in
   big cities.

5. The subway is _____ *faster* _____ (fast) than the bus.

C. CREATE Complete each sentence with the correct superlative form of the adjective in parentheses and your own opinions. Then discuss your answers with a partner.

1. _*Basketball*_ is _the most interesting_ (interesting) sport to watch.

2. _*Pinapple*_ is _the most delicious_ (delicious) food in the world.

3. _*Sumer*_ is _the most beautiful_ (beautiful) season of the year.

4. _*JuJithu*_ is _the most difficult_ (difficult) sport to play.

5. _*Tokyo*_ is _the most famous_ (famous) place in my country.

iQ PRACTICE   Go online for more practice with comparative and superlative adjectives. *Practice > Unit 5 > Activities 11–12*

My writing is much better than listening. (margin note)

UNIT ASSIGNMENT Write a plan for a family business

OBJECTIVE ▶

In this assignment, you will write a plan for a new family business. Your plan will include information about your new business, the services it will provide, and the jobs that the members of your family will do. As you prepare to write your plan, think about the Unit Question, "What makes a family business successful?" Use information from Reading 1, Reading 2, the unit video, and your work in the unit to support your writing. Refer to the Self-Assessment checklist on page 120.

iQ PRACTICE Go online to the Writing Tutor to read a model plan for a family business. *Practice ˃ Unit 5 ˃ Activity 13*

PLAN AND WRITE

A. BRAINSTORM Freewrite to brainstorm ideas for your new family business. What are some possible businesses? What items will you sell or what services will you provide? Think about what jobs the members of your family will do. Write down as many ideas as you can.

WRITING TIP

When you are writing a plan, don't just think about what you would like to see. Think about your audience. What might readers want to know about your business?

B. PLAN Review your freewriting. Choose the business you want to write about. Then answer the questions.

1. What kind of business will it be? What kind of product or service will your business provide? Describe the store or service.

2. Who will your customers be?

3. Why will your business be different from others?

4. Which family members will work in your company? What will their jobs be?

5. Why should people come and buy from your company?

6. Why will your business be successful?

iQ RESOURCES Go online to download and complete the outline for your family business plan. *Resources ˃ Writing Tools ˃ Unit 5 ˃ Outline*

C. WRITE Use your planning notes to write your plan for a new family business.

iQ PRACTICE Go online to the Writing Tutor to write your assignment. *Practice ˃ Unit 5 ˃ Activity 14*

1. Write your topic sentence first. Make sure the topic sentence introduces the main idea of the paragraph.

2. Be sure to use examples to support your main idea.

3. Be sure that each sentence is relevant and contributes to the main idea.

4. Look at the Self-Assessment checklist to guide your writing.

REVISE AND EDIT

iQ RESOURCES Go online to download the peer review worksheet.
Resources > Writing Tools > Unit 5 > Peer Review Worksheet

A. PEER REVIEW Read your partner's plan. Then use the peer review worksheet. Discuss the review with your partner.

B. REWRITE Based on your partner's review, revise and rewrite your plan.

C. EDIT Complete the Self-Assessment checklist as you prepare to write the final draft of your plan. Be prepared to hand in your work or discuss it in class.

SELF-ASSESSMENT	Yes	No
Do the sentences in your paragraph support the topic sentence?	☐	☐
Do you use transition words to unify the plan and help your ideas flow smoothly?	☐	☐
Underline any comparative or superlative adjectives. Are they in the correct form?	☐	☐
Is each word used correctly? Check a dictionary if you are not sure.	☐	☐
Does the plan include vocabulary from the unit?	☐	☐
Did you check the plan for punctuation, spelling, and grammar.	☐	☐

D. REFLECT Discuss these questions with a partner or group.

1. What is something new you learned in this unit?

2. Look back at the Unit Question—What makes a family business successful? Is your answer different now than when you started the unit? If yes, how is it different? Why?

iQ PRACTICE Go to the online discussion board to discuss the questions.
Practice > Unit 5 > Activity 15

TRACK YOUR SUCCESS

iQ PRACTICE Go online to check the words and phrases you have learned in this unit. *Practice > Unit 5 > Activity 16*

Check (✓) the skills you learned. If you need more work on a skill, refer to the page(s) in parentheses.

READING	☐ I can skim a text. (p. 101)
CRITICAL THINKING	☐ I can draw conclusions from various sources. (p. 111)
VOCABULARY	☐ I can use the dictionary to understand grammatical information. (p. 113)
WRITING	☐ I can write a paragraph with unified ideas. (p. 114)
GRAMMAR	☐ I can use comparative and superlative adjectives correctly. (pp. 117)

OBJECTIVE ▶ ☐ I can gather information and ideas to write a plan for a successful family business.

Brain Science

6

READING	identifying the author's purpose
CRITICAL THINKING	predicting topics and ideas
VOCABULARY	using the dictionary
WRITING	describing a process
GRAMMAR	infinitives of purpose

 UNIT QUESTION

How can you learn faster and better?

A. Discuss these questions with your classmates.

1. If you could improve the way that you learn, what would you choose to improve?

2. Some students seem to learn more easily than others. Why do you think this is?

3. Look at the photo. What are the people doing? Do you learn better in groups or by yourself?

B. Listen to *The Q Classroom* online. Then answer these questions.

1. Which student wants to improve his reading in English? What does he want to improve?

2. Which student wants to improve her listening in English? What does she want to be able to do better?

3. Think about the issues that the students discussed. Which student is most like you?

iQ PRACTICE Go to the online discussion board to discuss the Unit Question with your classmates. *Practice > Unit 6 > Activity 1*

UNIT OBJECTIVE ▶ Read the articles. Gather information and ideas to write a paragraph describing the steps of a process.

READING

READING 1

OBJECTIVE ▶

You Can Read Faster and Better

You are going to read a blog post about how to read faster. Use the blog post to gather information and ideas for your Unit Assignment.

VOCABULARY SKILL REVIEW

In Unit 4, you learned to use the dictionary to find additional information about words. Look up the words *benefit* and *provide*. Which prepositions are often used with these words? Which prepositions are used with them if you change the part of speech?

PREVIEW THE READING

A. VOCABULARY Here are some words from Reading 1. Read their definitions. Then complete each sentence.

---

automatically *(adverb)* 🔑 done in a way (like a machine) that does not require human control

benefit *(verb)* 🔑 OPAL to have a good or useful effect

comfort zone *(noun phrase)* a place or situation in which a person feels comfortable and not stressed

decrease *(verb)* 🔑 OPAL to become or to make something smaller or less

interact *(verb)* OPAL to communicate or mix with

pace *(noun)* 🔑 the speed at which you do something or at which something happens

process *(verb)* OPAL to deal with information

provide *(verb)* 🔑 OPAL to give or supply something to somebody

skip *(verb)* to leave something out; to not read or talk about something and move to the next part

unique *(adjective)* 🔑 OPAL not like anything else

🔑 Oxford 3000™ words   OPAL Oxford Phrasal Academic Lexicon

1. Students _____benefit_____ from having laptops: they can study anywhere.

2. At the bank, a machine ___automatically___ sorts and counts coins.

3. Ken decided to _____skip_____ the chapter he was reading because it was so boring.

4. I am waiting for prices to ___decrease___ before I buy a new phone.

5. If you want to succeed, you need to get out of your ___comfort zone___ .

6. It took a little time for Anya to ___process___ the bad news.

7. My brother is good with children. He likes to ___interact___ with them.

8. Run at a slower ___pace___ , and you won't get tired so quickly.

9. The school librarians are very helpful. They ___provide___ us with a lot of useful information.

10. The Grand Canyon is a ___unique___ place, I've never seen anywhere like it!

iQ PRACTICE Go online for more practice with the vocabulary.
Practice > Unit 6 > Activities 2–3

TIP FOR SUCCESS

Before you read a text, look at the title, photos, and format of the text. Think about what kind of information it might contain.

B. PREVIEW Quickly read the title of the blog post. Read the headings of the sections of the blog post. What do you think the blog post will be about?

C. QUICK WRITE What do you do when you read a new text? What skills and strategies do you use to try to understand the reading? Be sure to use this section for your Unit Assignment.

WORK WITH THE READING

A. INVESTIGATE Read the blog post and gather information about reading faster and better.

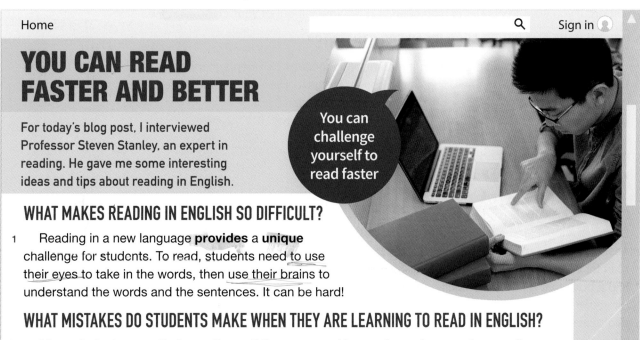

Home ⚲ Sign in 👤

YOU CAN READ FASTER AND BETTER

For today's blog post, I interviewed Professor Steven Stanley, an expert in reading. He gave me some interesting ideas and tips about reading in English.

You can challenge yourself to read faster

WHAT MAKES READING IN ENGLISH SO DIFFICULT?

1   Reading in a new language **provides** a **unique** challenge for students. To read, students need to use their eyes to take in the words, then use their brains to understand the words and the sentences. It can be hard!

WHAT MISTAKES DO STUDENTS MAKE WHEN THEY ARE LEARNING TO READ IN ENGLISH?

2   Many students move their mouths as if they are speaking each word, even when reading silently. This is a not a good idea because your eyes and brain can move faster than your mouth.

3   Another common problem is stopping to look up the meaning of every new word. You can **skip** over those words and still understand a lot of the reading. Or, just quickly underline the word as you read; then come back later to look it up in the dictionary. It also slows you down if you translate everything from English to your own language.

I SEE. ARE THERE OTHER PROBLEMS THAT STUDENTS HAVE?

4   Lots of students, especially when they are beginning, read just one word at a time. This **decreases** their reading speed. Don't read every word one by one. Instead, read in small groups of words or phrases that contain meaning. Here's an example of a sentence shown in thought groups. If you focus—on groups of words—together in thought groups—it is easier for your brain—to **process** the information. Reading faster can actually help you remember better. Your brain can understand groups of ideas better than just single words. Your goal should be to read **automatically** so that you can do it without thinking about individual words.

HOW ELSE CAN STUDENTS READ FASTER AND BETTER?

5   For one thing, students can **benefit** from practicing to increase their reading speed. Here's how. Use a book that is not too difficult for you. Select a page or two from the book. Read the passage to see how long it takes you. Then go back and read the same passage again. Can you beat[1] your time? What if you try again? If you do this, you should be able to increase your reading speed. It will help you see what it feels like to read more quickly.

6   Another way to read faster is to set a fast **pace** for yourself. Use your hand, a pencil, or a piece of paper to move quickly down the page. Then try to follow it with your eyes. It should be a little bit difficult to keep up. If it is too easy or feels very comfortable, then try increasing the speed. You want to provide yourself with a challenge. Think of reading faster as if it is a sport. If you want to get better, you need to push yourself out of your **comfort zone.**

DO YOU HAVE ANY OTHER GOOD IDEAS FOR STUDENTS?

7   Yes! For textbooks and more difficult material, I suggest that students mark up their books. By that, I mean that—as long as the book belongs to you—you shouldn't be afraid to write in it. Use a pen, pencil, or highlighter[2]. You can underline or highlight new vocabulary words and the main ideas. If you have questions or ideas, don't be afraid to write them in the margins of the book. Good readers like to **interact** with the text, and writing is a good way to do this.

8   Finally, students can improve their English by making reading a habit. Students should read every day. The best idea is to read for pleasure—to read for enjoyment. The secret is to find a book that is not too difficult for you. If it is too hard, then you might be discouraged. You should also read books about things that are really interesting to you. That will help you stay interested in the subject matter.

Highlighting or marking up your text can help with comprehension

[1]**beat:** to do better than someone or something
[2]**highlighter:** a special colored pen that goes on top of writing in a book to show that something is important

B. IDENTIFY Circle the ideas that the blog post includes.

1. Moving your mouth when you read can make you read more slowly.

2. It is important to understand every word in a reading passage.

3. It can be helpful for your English to read books that are easy for you.

4. It's good to practice your reading on subjects you don't like.

C. CATEGORIZE Read the statements. Write *T* (true) or *F* (false). Then correct each false statement to make it true. Write the paragraph number where the answer is found.

____ 1. Reading in English can be difficult.

   Paragraph:____ _____

____ 2. It's a good idea to pronounce each word as you read it.

   Paragraph:____ _____

____ 3. You should stop and look up the meaning of any words that you don't know.

   Paragraph:____ _____

____ 4. Translating everything from English to your own language will help you read faster.

   Paragraph:____ _____

____ 5. It is better to read in thought groups instead of one word at a time.

   Paragraph:____ _____

____ 6. It is good to practice reading faster, even if you feel uncomfortable.

   Paragraph:____ _____

____ 7. Reading for pleasure and enjoyment is a good way to improve your reading.

   Paragraph:____ _____

D. RESTATE Answer the questions. Use information from the reading.

1. Why is reading a unique challenge?

_____

2. What mistakes do students make when they are learning to read in English?

_____

3. Why is it better to read in thought groups instead of individual words?

_____

4. How would you go about pacing yourself to increase your reading speed?

_____

5. What is a good way for readers to interact with the text?

_____

E. SYNTHESIZE Look back at your Quick Write on page 125. How can you read faster and better? Add any new ideas or information you learned from the reading.

iQ PRACTICE   Go online for additional reading and comprehension.
Practice > Unit 6 > Activity 4

? WRITE WHAT YOU THINK

A. DISCUSS Discuss these questions in a group.

1. Do you have any of the same problems as described in the reading? Which ones?

2. The professor recommends writing in your books. Do you think this is a good idea? Why or why not?

3. Have you tried using any of the ideas to improve your reading? Which ones did you try? What happened?

B. COMPOSE Choose one of the questions and write a response. Look back at your Quick Write on page 125 as you think about what you learned.

Question: _____

My Response: _____

_____

_____

_____

The **purpose** of a text is the reason the author writes it. For example, the purpose of a newspaper article is to inform or give the reader information about something. The purpose of a letter to the newspaper is usually to express an opinion about something. As you read, look at the words the author uses, and ask yourself questions to help you identify the purpose. Here are some questions you can ask yourself as you read:

- Is the author trying to give me information about something?
- Is the author expressing his or her opinion about something?
- Is the author telling me a personal story?
- Is the author trying to make me interested or excited about something?
- Is the author trying to make me laugh?

Identifying the author's purpose can help you better understand the text you are reading.

A. INTERPRET Look back at Reading 1 on pages 125–126. What is the author's purpose? Circle two answers.

a. to tell a story

b. to make someone laugh

c. to give information

d. encourage the reader

B. IDENTIFY Read the titles. Look at the words the authors use. Then match each title with the correct purpose.

_____ 1. "My Embarrassing Adventures with Technology"

_____ 2. "Competitive Sports Are Too Competitive"

_____ 3. "My Grandfather's Childhood in Egypt"

_____ 4. "New Research Shows Birds See More Colors"

_____ 5. "You Can Be Stronger in Two Weeks!"

a. to tell a story

b. to make someone laugh

c. to express an opinion

d. to make someone interested in something

e. to give information

iQ PRACTICE Go online for more practice with identifying the author's purpose. *Practice > Unit 6 > Activity 5*

CRITICAL THINKING STRATEGY

Predicting topics and ideas

Before you read, it is a good idea to make guesses about what the reading is about. These guesses are called predictions. Making predictions will make you think about a text and can help you understand and remember more. Skim the reading and ask yourself some questions.

What kind of reading is it? (article, report, blog, etc.)

Read the title and any subheadings—what are the important words?

Are there any pictures or diagrams? What do they show?

What do you already know about the topic?

Now, use the information to make predictions. Here are examples for Reading 1:

1. *The reading is a blog post, and the topic is how to improve your reading in English.*
2. *The author is positive about the topic.*
3. *The reading includes information on what the brain does when we read.*
4. *The reading includes advice such as using a dictionary to help you understand.*

Use your predictions to test your understanding of the reading. Were your predictions correct? You can write down the answers about your predictions to see if you were right. Here are answers for the predictions about Reading 1.

1. Correct. 2. Correct. 3. Correct. 4. Incorrect—using a dictionary slows you down. You should practice to make yourself read faster.

iQ PRACTICE   Go online to watch the Critical Thinking Video and check your comprehension. *Practice > Unit 6 > Activity 8*

A. APPLY Skim Reading 2 on pages 132–133. Answer the questions.

1. What kind of reading is it?

2. What are the important words in the title and subheadings?

3. What do the pictures show?

B. SYNTHESIZE Use the information from Activity A to make predictions about the reading. When you read the text for Work With the Reading, check if your predictions were correct or not. Correct any mistakes.

Prediction 1: _____ Correct? Y/N

Prediction 2: _____ Correct? Y/N

Prediction 3: _____ Correct? Y/N

Brain Secrets of the Most Successful Students

You are going to read a magazine article about the brain and good study habits. Use the article to gather information and ideas for your Unit Assignment.

VOCABULARY SKILL REVIEW

In Unit 5, you learned about grammatical information in the dictionary. Look at the vocabulary on this page and on page 124. Using a dictionary, find out which nouns are countable, which are uncountable, and which can be either countable or uncountable.

PREVIEW THE READING

A. VOCABULARY Here are some words from Reading 2. Read their definitions. Then complete each sentence.

access *(verb)* OPAL to get or use something

assist *(verb)* 🔑 to help

concept *(noun)* 🔑 OPAL an idea; a basic principle

eventually *(adverb)* 🔑 after a long time

frustrated *(adjective)* angry or impatient because you cannot do or achieve what you want to do

internal *(adjective)* 🔑 OPAL of or on the inside of a person, place, or object

period *(noun)* 🔑 OPAL a length of time

physical *(adjective)* 🔑 OPAL of and for your body

productive *(adjective)* OPAL that can make or grow something well or in large quantities

respond *(verb)* 🔑 OPAL to say or do something as an answer or reaction to something

🔑 Oxford 3000™ words   OPAL Oxford Phrasal Academic Lexicon

ACADEMIC LANGUAGE

The word *concept* has the same meaning as *idea*, but *concept* is used more often in academic writing. Choose your words carefully to make your writing sound more academic.

─────────────| OPAL
Oxford Phrasal Academic Lexicon

1. I thought my friends would never come back from the store, but _eventually_ they did.

2. Michael got a lot of work done. It was a very _productive_ day.

3. You can _access_ the school Wi-Fi using this password.

4. At our store, the computer specialists _assist_ customers. It's their job.

5. To be healthy, it is important to develop _physical_ strength.

6. The doctor couldn't see anything wrong on the outside. It was an _internal_ problem. _inside_

7. I tried to register for classes today, but the website didn't work! Now all the classes I want are full. I'm so _frustrated_.

8. The _period_ of the 1920s was known as the Jazz Age.

9. The phone company said they would _respond_ quickly to my problem.

10. The idea of death is a difficult _concept_ to understand.

iQ PRACTICE Go online for more practice with the vocabulary.
Practice > Unit 6 > Activities 6–7

B. PREVIEW Look at the magazine article. Where do the students come from?

C. QUICK WRITE Most teachers and parents tell you to study hard. How could you study so that your studying could be easier? Be sure to use this section for your Unit Assignment.

WORK WITH THE READING

A. INVESTIGATE Read the magazine article and gather information about secrets of successful students.

BRAIN SECRETS OF THE MOST SUCCESSFUL STUDENTS

1   Students everywhere wonder how they can study less and learn more. Fortunately, thanks to advances in the field of brain science, it is possible for everyone to be a more successful student. Here are study tips from four successful students.

YUKI TANAKA FROM JAPAN

2   I find it's really helpful to study for short **periods** of time and then take a break. If I try to study for a long time, my brain doesn't have a chance to rest. But if I work for about 45 minutes and then stop for a little while, I actually become more **productive**.

3   Here's a good way to remember new information. Instead of trying to remember something new by just studying it once, I return to it a few different times and repeat it. So if I am trying to learn new vocabulary words, first I try to remember them right after I learn them. That way my brain can **access** the new information. Then I try to remember them again the next day. And then again the day after that. By putting some space in between, I can **assist** my brain to remember the new words.

Yuki Tanaka tries to remember new vocabulary

EMRE ARSLAN FROM TURKEY

4 Believe it or not, the best advice that I got to increase my brain power actually came from my mother! She always told me to be sure to get enough sleep at night. It turns out that my mom was right! Scientists say getting enough sleep is important to help your brain work at a high level. During the day, your brain gets filled with information. At night, when you sleep, your brain continues to process that information. Scientists found that enough healthy sleep can increase people's ability to learn. But when people don't get enough sleep, they don't learn as well.

5 OK, here's another tip from my mom: it's important to get enough exercise. When you exercise, you increase the movement of blood all through your body. This includes your brain. When your brain receives more blood, it can grow new **internal** pathways[1] to help you think better. Thanks, Mom! I'm going to go and work out now!

Emre Arslan tries to get enough exercise

SARAH COOPER FROM CANADA

6 The key for me is to take notes in class. Writing something down helps me remember, and I need to understand something in order to write it down. There is something about the **physical act** of writing that helps me remember the ideas better. When I first tried to take notes, I felt **frustrated.** But I kept trying, and **eventually** my listening and comprehension skills got better. So that has worked really well for me. Also, I heard that researchers said that if you are taking notes in class, it is better to use a pen and paper rather than a laptop. In experiments, when students took notes by hand, they listened more actively and were better able to identify important **concepts**.

Sarah Cooper takes notes in class

ALEX LUKANOV FROM RUSSIA

7 My secret to success is to give my brain some variety. If I try to learn everything the same way every time, my brain won't find it interesting. So instead of always studying the same way, I introduce some variety into my study habits. So if I usually study in my bedroom, I try studying in the kitchen instead. Rather than studying only in the evening, I try studying during the afternoon. My brain **responds** well to things that are new.

8 Another thing that helps me is to try to teach another student. When I take the time to study and then explain ideas to another person, it really helps me understand the subject and organize my ideas. When I am able to successfully teach another person, it helps me remember and process the information, too.

9 Try out some of these ideas. You may find that you can study less and learn more!

[1]**pathways:** connections

Alex Lukanov teaches another student

B. IDENTIFY What is the main advice that Yuki gives?

☐ 1. It is important to get enough sleep.

☐ 2. Writing something down helps you remember.

☑ 3. A good way to remember is study something and then repeat the process.

☐ 4. It's helpful to teach another person.

C. CATEGORIZE Read the statements. Write *T* (true) or *F* (false). Then correct each false statement to make it true. Write the paragraph number where the answer is found.

_T_ 1. It is helpful to study for short periods of time and then take a break.

Paragraph: _2_ _____

_F_ 2. Yuki suggests trying to remember something one time. by stoding it once

Paragraph: _3_ She returns to it a different time neive

_F_ 3. It doesn't matter how much sleep you get. your study

Paragraph: _4_ getting enght sleep is important to kept.

_T_ 4. Your brain receives more blood from exercise.

Paragraph: _5_ _____

_T_ 5. Taking notes by hand helps students understand concepts.

Paragraph: _6_ _____

_F_ 6. Alex likes to study in the same way each time. habit

Paragraph: _7_ He intioduces some variety in his stull

_T_ 7. Explaining ideas to another person can help organize the subject in your head.

Paragraph: _8_ _____

D. CATEGORIZE Match the student with the advice they give. Write the name of the student next to the advice.

Yuki   Emre   Sarah   Alex

_E_ 1. Get enough exercise.

_S_ 2. Take notes in class.

_Y_ 3. Study for short periods; then take a break.

_A_ 4. Try to teach another person.

_E_ 5. Get enough sleep.

_A_ 6. Give your brain some variety.

E. DISCUSS Discuss the questions in a group.

1. Which person in Reading 2 do you agree with? Why?

2. Do you think the information in Reading 2 will help you become a better learner? Or will you keep studying in the same way?

3. How much help should teachers give students in their classes? How much is it the responsibility of the student?

WORK WITH THE VIDEO

VIDEO VOCABULARY

balance (n.) the ability to keep steady with an equal amount of weight on each side of the body

function (n.) the purpose of something or someone

impressive (adj.) causing a feeling of admiration and respect because of importance/ size/excellent quality

unconscious (adj.) existing or happening without you realizing; not deliberate

A. PREVIEW What functions do you think your brain controls? Check all that apply.

Cerebrum

Brain Stem

Spinal Cord

Cerebellum

☐ thinking   ☐ sleeping   ☐ heart rate   ☐ personality

iQ RESOURCES Go online to watch the video about the brain.
Resources > Video > Unit 6 > Unit Video

B. CATEGORIZE Watch the video two or three times. What functions or processes does each part of the brain control?

Part of the brain	Processes or functions
brain stem	
cerebellum	
cerebrum	

C. EXTEND Think about the different parts of the brain. Which part is the most important to help you learn a new language?

WRITE WHAT YOU THINK

SYNTHESIZE Think about Reading 1, Reading 2, and the unit video as you discuss these questions. Then choose one question and write a response.

WRITING TIP
When you write a paragraph in response to a question, begin with a topic sentence. Support your ideas with reasons, supporting details, and examples. End with a strong concluding sentence.

1. What advice would you give to a younger person who is hoping to improve his or her grades?

2. Consider your own reading and study habits. What do you think you could do differently to improve your learning?

VOCABULARY SKILL Using the dictionary

Words with more than one meaning

Many words have more than one meaning, or definition, even if they are spelled and pronounced the same way. Using a dictionary can help you identify the correct meaning of a new word. If a word has two definitions that are the same part of speech (*noun, verb, adjective, adverb*), they will likely appear under the same entry in the dictionary. If the two meanings are different parts of speech, they might appear under different entries in the dictionary.

light¹ /laɪt/ *noun* **1** [C, U] the energy from the sun, a lamp, etc. that allows you to see things: *a beam/ray of light • the light of the sun • The light was too bad for us to read by.* **2** [C] something that produces light, for example, an electric lamp: *Suddenly, all the lights came on/went out. • the lights of the city in the distance • a neon light • That car's lights aren't on. • Please switch the lights off before you leave.*

light² /laɪt/ *adj.*
> **NOT DARK 1** having a lot of light: *In the summer it's still light at 9 o'clock. • a light room* **ANT** dark
> **OF A COLOR 2** pale in color: *a light blue sweater* **ANT** dark
> **NOT HEAVY 3** not of great weight: *Carry this bag – it's the lightest. • I've lost weight – I'm five pounds lighter than I used to be. • light clothes (= for summer)* **ANT** heavy

You can improve your vocabulary by using a dictionary to look up words with more than one meaning.

All dictionary entries adapted from the *Oxford American Dictionary for learners of English* © Oxford University Press 2011.

A. APPLY Use your dictionary to find the different definitions of the words below. Then write the definition and the sentence that uses the word in context. Compare your answers with a partner.

1. light

   Definition 1: _the energy from the sun, a lamp, etc._

   Sentence: _The light was too low for us to see._

   Definition 2: _something that produces light, for example, an electric lamp_

   Sentence: _Suddenly, all the lights came on._

   Definition 3: _____

   Sentence: _____

   Definition 4: _____

   Sentence: _____

2. row

   Definition 1: _____

   Sentence: _____

   Definition 2: _____

   Sentence: _____

Rowing

3. tip

Definition 1: _____

Sentence: _____

Definition 2: _____

Sentence: _____

Definition 3: _____

Sentence: _____

4. bank

Definition 1: _____

Sentence: _____

Definition 2: _____

Sentence: _____

Definition 3: _____

Sentence: _____

TIP FOR SUCCESS
Sometimes words
with more than one
meaning are spelled
the same way, but
they are pronounced
differently. Pay attention
to the different
pronunciations for the
different meanings
of *record* and *wind*.

B. IDENTIFY Work with a partner. Look up the words *record* and *wind* in the dictionary. Answer the questions below.

1. How many definitions are there for the word *record*? _____

2. How many of the definitions did you already know? _____

3. How many definitions are there for the word *wind*? _____

4. How many of the definitions did you already know? _____

iQ PRACTICE Go online for more practice with using the dictionary.
Practice ❯ Unit 6 ❯ Activity 9

In 2019, Thailand set a Guinness World Record for the largest serving of mango sticky rice.

WRITING

OBJECTIVE ▶ At the end of this unit, you will write a paragraph describing the steps of a process. This paragraph will include specific information from the readings and your own ideas.

WRITING SKILL Describing a process

When you write about a **process**, you describe how to do something step-by-step. First, you write a topic sentence that states what the process is. Then you explain each step clearly. Use **time order** words to help guide your reader. Time order words usually come at the beginning of a sentence and are followed by a comma. Note that *then* is not followed by a comma.

first	next	then	later	after that	finally

TIP FOR SUCCESS
Use several different time order words in your writing. This will help make your writing more interesting to the reader.

⎡ **First,** get out your dictionary.
⎣ **Then** look up the words.

Use these time order words to link two steps in a process.

⎣ after   as soon as   before   when   while

⎡ **Before** you begin to read, check your watch.
⎣ **While** you are reading, highlight the important ideas.

A. WRITING MODEL Read the model instructions for doing math homework. Circle the time order words.

Here's how to do your math homework. First, get out your textbook or worksheet and look up your assignment. Then carefully read the directions. Next, start to work on the math problems. When you get stuck on a problem, don't be afraid to ask for help. While you are finishing your homework, be careful not to make mistakes. Finally, check your work before you hand it in to your teacher.

B. IDENTIFY Read the steps about how to write a paragraph. Then write the steps in the flow chart on page 140 to show the correct order.

a. Write a conclusion.

b. Check your spelling.

c. Proofread your work.

d. Brainstorm your ideas.

e. Check your grammar.

f. Write supporting sentences.

g. Write a good topic sentence.

Process: How to write a paragraph

Start

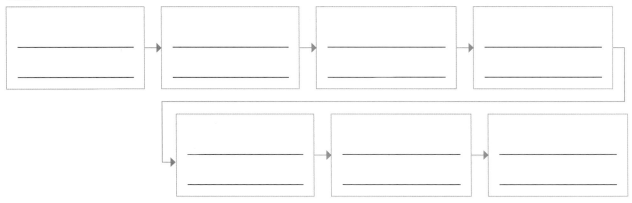

Finish

C. APPLY Write the process from Activity B in a paragraph, using time order words. You may combine two steps into one sentence.

D. SYNTHESIZE Think of a process that describes something that you know how to do, make, fix, or use. Then write notes for the steps in the flow chart. Add more boxes if you need to.

Process: _____

Start

Finish

E. DISCUSS Show your flow chart to a partner and explain the steps. Answer any questions about the process. Do you need to add additional steps or information? Add notes to your chart.

F. EXPLAIN What are some things that sometimes go wrong in your process? What are some extra tips you can include? Complete the sentences on page 141 to give additional information about the process.

1. When you _____ going to 2 Gym 3 timed week _____, be sure that you
   _____ should choose days _____.

2. Be careful when you _____ go to a gym _____ more than 3 times a week _____ because sometimes
   _____ you feel tired _____.

3. Don't forget to _____ take a rest day _____. You will
   _____ get tird easyer _____ if you don't _____ take a rest _____.

G. COMPOSE Use your flow chart and one or two sentences from activity F to write a paragraph describing a process. Make sure to use time order words.

iQ PRACTICE Go online for more practice with describing a process.
Practice > Unit 6 > Activity 10

GRAMMAR Infinitives of purpose

An **infinitive** is *to* + the base form of a verb. We sometimes use infinitives to show the purpose of an action. We call these **infinitives of purpose**. An infinitive of purpose is usually separated from the main verb in a sentence. Infinitives of purpose can be used with most action verbs.

Get enough sleep **to increase** your brain power.
main verb | infinitive of purpose

You can **pace** yourself **to read** faster.
main verb | infinitive of purpose

Skip unknown words **to speed up** your reading.
main verb | infinitive of purpose

Sometimes an infinitive of purpose comes before the main verb.

To increase your brain power, **get** enough sleep.
infinitive of purpose | main verb

Not all infinitives are infinitives of purpose. An infinitive of purpose has the same meaning as *in order to*. If you insert the phrase *in order to*, it will help you figure out if an infinitive is one that shows purpose.

Infinitive of purpose:

⌈ He called me **to apologize**.
⌊ He called me **in order to apologize**. (same meaning)

Not an infinitive of purpose:

⌈ He called me and said that he wanted **to apologize**.
⌊ He called me and said that he wanted **in order to apologize**. (not the same meaning and incorrect)

iQ RESOURCES Go online to watch the Grammar Skill Video.
Resources > Video > Unit 6 > Grammar Skill Video

A. IDENTIFY Circle each infinitive of purpose in the paragraph. Remember, not every infinitive shows purpose.

Creating your own online blog is a good way to connect with people who share your interests. I started a blog last year (to share) my experience as an international exchange student in Miami, Florida. It was very easy to do, and it allowed me to practice my writing skills and be in touch with other students. Here's how you do it. First, go online to find free blog websites. There are many available, but you should look for one that is easy to use. Start by looking at some sample blogs to get ideas for your own blog. Then get started! The site will tell you what to do for each step of the set-up process. After you have set up your blog, you can write your first post. Use photos to add visual interest to your page. Having a blog is a fun experience because you get comments from people who read it. It's also a great way to practice your writing skills and to think creatively.

B. APPLY Answer these questions using infinitives of purpose.

1. Why do you use the Internet?

_____

2. What is another kind of technology that you use? Why do you use it?

_____

3. Why do students want to read faster?

_____

4. Why are you studying English?

_____

iQ PRACTICE   Go online for more practice with infinitives of purpose.
Practice > _Unit 6_ > _Activities 11–12_

UNIT ASSIGNMENT

OBJECTIVE ▶

Write a paragraph describing a process

In this assignment, you will write a paragraph describing a process. As you prepare your paragraph, think about the Unit Question, "How can you learn faster and better?" Use information from Reading 1, Reading 2, the unit video, and your work in this unit to support your paragraph. Refer to the Self-Assessment checklist on page 144.

iQ PRACTICE   Go online to the Writing Tutor to read a model paragraph describing a process. _Practice_ > _Unit 6_ > _Activity 13_

PLAN AND WRITE

A. BRAINSTORM Use the chart to brainstorm ideas for a topic. Then share your ideas with a partner. Decide which topics are the most interesting.

Learning new vocabulary words	Reading and understanding a new book	Studying for a test

B. PLAN Complete the activities.

1. Look at your chart in Activity A and select a topic for your paragraph.

2. Think about how you will explain the steps of the process. Make a flow chart of the steps in order. Then make a list of time order words you can use to connect the steps of your process.

iQ RESOURCES   Go online to download and complete the outline for your paragraph describing a process. _Resources_ > _Writing Tools_ > _Unit 6_ > _Outline_

C. WRITE Use your planning notes to write your paragraph.

1. Write a topic sentence for your paragraph. Then use your notes from Activity B to write your paragraph. Use time order words from the Writing Skill on page 139. Use infinitives of purpose where you can. Include sentences with additional tips and information about what can go wrong.

2. Look at the Self-Assessment checklist to guide your writing.

iQ PRACTICE Go online to the Writing Tutor to write your assignment.
Practice > Unit 6 > Activity 14

REVISE AND EDIT

iQ RESOURCES Go online to download the peer review worksheet.
Resources > Writing Tools > Unit 6 > Peer Review Worksheet

A. PEER REVIEW Read a partner's paragraph. Then use the peer review worksheet. Discuss the review with your partner.

B. REWRITE Based on your partner's review, revise and rewrite your paragraph.

C. EDIT Complete the Self-Assessment checklist as you prepare to write the final draft of your paragraph. Be prepared to hand in your work or discuss it in class.

SELF-ASSESSMENT	Yes	No
Do you describe the process clearly using time order words?	☐	☐
Does your paragraph include infinitives of purpose?	☐	☐
Is each word spelled correctly? Check a dictionary if you are not sure.	☐	☐
Does the paragraph include vocabulary from the unit?	☐	☐
Did you check the paragraph for punctuation, spelling, and grammar?	☐	☐

D. REFLECT Discuss these questions with a partner or group.

1. What is something new you learned in this unit?

2. Look back at the Unit Question—How can you learn faster and better? Is your answer different now than when you started the unit? If yes, how is it different? Why?

iQ PRACTICE Go to the online discussion board to discuss these questions.
Practice > Unit 6 > Activity 15

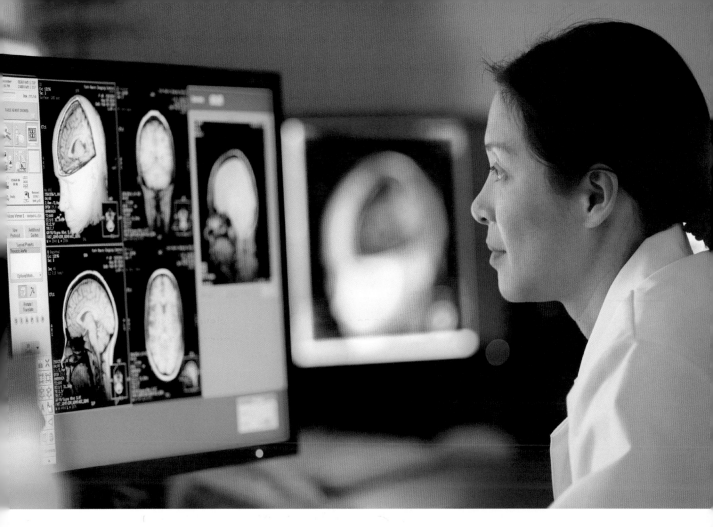

TRACK YOUR SUCCESS

iQ PRACTICE Go online to check the words and phrases you have learned in this unit. *Practice > Unit 6 > Activity 16*

Check (✓) the skills you learned. If you need more work on a skill, refer to the page(s) in parentheses.

READING	☐ I can identify the author's purpose. (p. 129)
CRITICAL THINKING	☐ I can predict topics and ideas (p. 130)
VOCABULARY	☐ I can use the dictionary to identify the correct meanings of words. (p. 136)
WRITING	☐ I can describe a step-by-step process. (p. 139)
GRAMMAR	☐ I can use infinitives of purpose correctly. (p. 141)

OBJECTIVE ▶ ☐ I can gather information and ideas to write a paragraph describing the steps of a process.

Environmental
Science

READING   identifying claims and support
VOCABULARY   phrasal verbs
WRITING   using sentence variety
GRAMMAR   simple past and past continuous
CRITICAL THINKING   analyzing and evaluating ideas

UNIT QUESTION

Do cities need nature?

A Discuss these questions with your classmates.

1. Nature includes everything in our world that is not made by humans, such as plants and animals. What nature can you find in your city or town? For example, are there parks, lakes, rivers, or gardens? Are there wild animals? Make a list.

2. Look at the photo. Do you think that cities need nature? Why or why not?

B Listen to *The Q Classroom* online. Then answer these questions.

1. What examples of nature in a city did the students give?

2. Did the students agree about the importance of nature in the city? Explain.

3. Do you think nature is important in a city? Why or why not?

iQ PRACTICE Go to the online discussion board to discuss the Unit Question with your classmates. *Practice > Unit 7 > Activity 1*

UNIT OBJECTIVE

Read the articles. Gather information and ideas to write an opinion paragraph about nature in a city.

READING

READING 1

OBJECTIVE ▶

Take a Nature Break

You are going to read an article about how nature affects people in a city. Use the article to gather information and ideas for your Unit Assignment.

PREVIEW THE READING

A. VOCABULARY Here are some words from Reading 1. Read the sentences. Then write each underlined word or phrase next to the correct definition.

1. I can count on my friends for <u>emotional</u> support when I'm sad or upset. *example*

2. Students who study all night are often <u>unable</u> to concentrate the next day. *opposite / cause ←→ effect*

3. After my <u>discussion</u> with my professor, I have <u>a better understanding of</u> the assignment. *cause ←→ effect*

4. Omar has a very positive <u>attitude</u>. He is always <u>cheerful and pleasant</u>. *example*

5. The first <u>experience</u> of visiting a different country is usually unforgettable. *example*

6. The researchers will <u>divide</u> the participants <u>into</u> three groups for the experiment. *similar*

7. Scientists <u>found that</u> teenagers who get an average of eight hours of sleep are <u>less stressed</u>. *cause ←→ effect*

8. Ana is very <u>generous</u> with her time. If you are having trouble with your homework, she will offer to help. *similar*

9. I like to <u>relax</u> after dinner. Usually I read or watch TV. *example*

10. Students <u>benefit from</u> working on projects <u>together</u>. *cause ←→ effect*

a. <u>divid into</u> *(verb phrase)* to separate into different parts

b. <u>emotional</u> *(adjective)* connected with people's feelings

c. <u>attitude</u> *(verb)* the way you think, <u>feel</u>, or <u>behave</u>

d. <u>find that</u> *(verb phrase)* discovered that something is true after trying it or testing it

e. <u>benefit from</u> *(verb phrase)* to be in a better position because of something

f. <u>relax</u> *(verb)* to spend time not doing very much

g. <u>experience</u> *(noun)* something that has happened to you

h. <u>generous</u> *(adjective)* willing to give more money, help, etc., than is usual

i. <u>unable</u> *(adjective)* not able to do something

j. <u>a better understand</u> *(noun phrase)* an improved state of knowing or realizing something

ACADEMIC LANGUAGE

The corpus shows that *found that* is often used in academic writing to describe the results of research or a study.

The researchers found that. . .

The engineer has found that the. . .

OPAL

Oxford Phrasal Academic Lexicon

iQ PRACTICE Go online for more practice with the vocabulary.
Practice › Unit 7 › Activities 2–3

B. PREVIEW Read the title of the article. Look at the photos. How are people relaxing in this city park?

C. QUICK WRITE Where is your favorite place to enjoy nature? Describe the place and how you feel when you are there. Write for five minutes. Be sure to use this section for your Unit Assignment.

WORK WITH THE READING

A. INVESTIGATE Read the article and gather information about the positive effects of nature in cities.

Title

topic

TAKE A NATURE BREAK

Introduction

1   Imagine that you live in a large city. You've had a stressful day. You need to **relax** and clear your mind[1]. Which of these would you choose?

a. Go out for dinner with friends.

b. Take a walk in a city park.

c. Play video games.

d. Work out at an indoor gym.

2   All of these are popular ways to relax and clear your mind, but only one will really help: Take a walk in a city park. Why is that? According to experts, it is

because when we are in nature, our emotions are more positive and our thinking is clearer.

3   Researchers at Stanford University in California did an experiment to find out how nature influences people (Bratman, et al, 2015). They **divided** 60 people **into** two groups. One group spent 50 minutes walking in a busy city. The other group spent 50 minutes walking in a natural area with trees and grass. They tested the people before and after their walks. The scientists **found that** after walking, the nature walkers showed different brain activity. Their brains showed less activity for negative

reason 1

Main Support

[1]**clear your mind:** become free of thoughts that worry or confuse you

w key words

emotions and less stress. In addition, those people did better on memory tests than the city walkers. It was clear that walking in nature made a difference.

4 Having **a better understanding of** the relationship between being in nature and mental health is important because more and more people live and work in large cities. Today, over 50% of the world's population lives in a city, and it will soon be 70%. Studies show that people living in cities have more mental health problems. City residents have more depression[2], anxiety[3], and stress than residents of small towns. Scientists believe it may be because city residents have less time in nature.

5 Nature influences city residents in other ways as well. According to studies at the University of Rochester, when people were in nature, they became more **generous** with their money and more interested in community. In other words, being in nature changed their behavior and **attitudes**. At the University of Pennsylvania, scientists found that creating green grassy areas made people feel safer and decreased crime. In addition, neighborhood parks encourage more physical activity and more social connections. Nature affects behavior of city residents in good ways. More nature in cities can result in stronger community connections, safer communities, and more physical activity.

6 Scientists want to know what kind of nature **experience** makes a difference. Researchers have found that you don't need to go to a large park to **benefit from** nature. City residents can benefit from small parks, streets with trees, and small green spaces. Even a short time in nature can give you a mental and **emotional** rest that will help you throughout the day. Noticing nature around you lets your mind rest.

7 So, the next time you feel tired, stressed, or **unable** to concentrate, take a short nature break. Take a walk or sit in a park, and notice the trees and sky. You may be surprised to find that a little nature makes a big difference.

[2]**depression:** a medical condition in which a person feels very sad and anxious
[3]**anxiety:** the state of feeling nervous or worried that something bad is going to happen

Reference
Bratman, G.N., Daily, G. C., Levy, B.J., & Gross, J.J. (2015, June) The benefits of nature experience: Improved affect and cognition. *Landscape and Urban Planning*, 138, 41–50. doi: https://doi.org/10.1016/j.landurbplan.2015.02.005

B. IDENTIFY Refer back to the reading as you answer these questions. Write the paragraph number where you found your answers. Then discuss your answers with a partner.

1. What are two things that researchers at Stanford University found out?

   Paragraph:____ _____

2. Why is it important to understand how nature affects city residents?

   Paragraph:____ _____

3. How did being in nature change people's behavior, according to researchers at the University of Rochester?

   Paragraph:____ _____

4. Do parks improve social connections between people?

   Paragraph:____ _____

5. Do you need to go to a large park to benefit from nature? Explain.

   Paragraph:____ _____

C. APPLY Complete the main idea statement. Use some of the words from the box and your own words.

city residents	in positive ways	parks
divides	influences	pollution
experience	notices	stressful

The main idea of this article is that nature _____.

A fact is something that people generally agree is true. A reader will accept some facts based on general knowledge. A claim is a statement presented as a fact. However, people may not agree with or believe a claim without support.

Cities have more pollution than most small towns. (This fact is general knowledge. People will generally agree it is true.)

City residents have more mental health problems. (This is a claim, and it is not supported. This statement needs to be supported by research or other facts.)

According to numerous studies, city residents have more mental health problems. (This claim is supported.)

When reading, it is important to identify the writer's claims and see if they are supported by facts or research.

iQ RESOURCES Go online to watch the Reading Skill Video.
Resources > Video > Unit 7 > Reading Skill Video

A. IDENTIFY Match each claim with the support given in the article. Write the paragraph number for the support.

_____ 1. Being in nature makes people more generous with their money.

_____ 2. More and more people are living in cities.

_____ 3. Walking 50 minutes in nature decreases stress and improves memory.

_____ 4. City residents have more mental health problems.

_____ 5. People felt safer when more grassy areas were added to their neighborhood.

a. This research was done at Stanford University.

   Paragraph _____

b. Fact: over 50% of the world's population lives in a city, and soon it will be 70%.

   Paragraph _____

c. This is supported by numerous studies.

   Paragraph _____

d. This experiment was done at the University of Pennsylvania.

   Paragraph _____

e. This is according to research done at the University of Rochester.

   Paragraph _____

B. IDENTIFY Read the paragraph and answer the questions.

Freeways are important for transportation in large cities, but sometimes, they bring too much traffic, noise, and pollution. This was true of the Cheonggye Freeway in Seoul, South Korea. Built in 1968, the freeway covered Cheonggye Creek. By the 1990s, the Cheonggye Freeway was a major urban problem. In the early 2000s, the city removed the freeway and started a new, fast bus service. Now a beautiful artificial creek flows through the city. It has helped the environment. It has also improved the tourist economy. Removing this major freeway has improved the quality of life for Seoul residents.

1. Underline the three claims that need support. Remember, a claim is a statement presented as a fact, which some people may not believe.

2. Read the facts below. Mark in the paragraph where you would insert each fact to support a claim.

   a. In fact, changes resulted in a 3.3 degree-Celsius drop in the average summer temperatures in the area near the creek, according to Congress for New Urbanism.

   b. It had the highest levels of noise and traffic in the city.

   c. About half a million people visit the creek each week, many of them tourists.

3. The final sentence of the paragraph does not need support. Why is that?

   a. The concluding sentence is summarizing ideas.

   b. It is a fact that will be generally accepted by the readers.

   c. There is no way to prove that quality of life has improved.

iQ PRACTICE Go online for more practice with identifying claims and support.
Practice > Unit 7 > Activity 4

C. EXTEND Answer the questions. Think about your own experience.

1. Do you think you would feel differently after walking for 50 minutes in nature compared with walking for 50 minutes in a busy city? Explain your answer.

   _____

2. What is the most surprising or interesting point in the article? Why?

   _____

3. In your opinion, does your city have enough places to experience nature? Explain your answer.

   _____

 iQ PRACTICE Go online for additional reading and comprehension.
Practice > Unit 7 > Activity 5

WRITE WHAT YOU THINK

A. DISCUSS Discuss the questions in a group.

1. What is your personal experience of being in nature? Give an example of a time when you were in nature. Describe how you felt during and after that time.

2. Do you think it as important for cities to have nature for residents as it is to have places for people to play sports such as soccer or baseball? What about playgrounds for children? What percentage of available space should be given to nature, sports, and playgrounds? Give reasons to support your answers.

B. SYNTHESIZE Choose one of the questions from Activity A and write a multiple-sentence response. Look back at your Quick Write on page 149 as you think about what you learned.

Question: _____

My response: _____

_____

_____

_____

Naturally Urban

You are going to read an article about three cities. Use the article to gather information and ideas for your Unit Assignment.

PREVIEW THE READING

A. VOCABULARY Here are some words from Reading 2. Read their definitions. Then complete each sentence.

> **ancient** *(adjective)* ⚿ very old
>
> **as a result** *(prepositional phrase)* OPAL something that happens because of something else
>
> **connected** *(adjective)* having a link between two things
>
> **government** *(noun)* ⚿ OPAL the group of people who rule or control a country or state
>
> **plant** *(verb)* ⚿ to put plants, seeds, etc., in the ground to grow
>
> **remarkable** *(adjective)* ⚿ unusual and surprising in a way that people notice
>
> **surround** *(verb)* ⚿ to be all around something or somebody
>
> **wildlife** *(noun)* ⚿ wild birds, plants, animals, etc.

⚿ Oxford 3000™ words   OPAL Oxford Phrasal Academic Lexicon

1. In this city, there are birds, but there isn't much other _____.

2. It is _____ that such an old city has such large, beautiful parks.

3. Because my cousin and I are the same age, we feel very _____.

4. The city has excellent public transportation. _____, many people can travel by train, subway, or bus.

5. The _____ requires all new stores to plant trees in front of their buildings.

6. After the new highway is finished, the state will ___plant___ trees and bushes along it.

7. Mountains ___surround___ the city. You can see them from anywhere in the city.

8. The ___ancient___ bridge needs many repairs. It's not safe to cross it.

iQ PRACTICE Go online for more practice with the vocabulary.
Practice ▶ Unit 7 ▶ Activities 6–7

TIP FOR SUCCESS
Before you read an
article, think about
what you already know
about the topic. Using
prior knowledge will
help you deepen your
understanding of the
text. What do you
know about Singapore,
Cairo, and Vancouver?

B. PREVIEW Look at photos and read the captions. What do the cities mentioned in the article have in common?

C. QUICK WRITE Describe what you see in one of the photos. How is nature part of this city? Write at least five sentences.

WORK WITH THE READING

A. INVESTIGATE Read the article and gather information about nature in these three cities.

NATURALLY URBAN

This huge garden is over 250 acres. It has over 100 different types of birds and 500,000 types of plants.

1 Singapore, Cairo, and Vancouver: three very different cities that have added more nature for their residents in unique ways. Can every city become a green city[1]? Read and decide for yourself.

SINGAPORE

2 Singapore is a small island nation. All of its people live in an urban area. With a population of over 5.6 million people, it is hard to believe that the city is the greenest, most environmentally friendly city in Asia. Because it is an island, the city cannot grow out. It can only grow up. Therefore, Singapore is a city of tall **skyscrapers**. However, the **government** requires all new buildings to have some plants. **As a result**, new buildings are often **connected** with other buildings by gardens or walking tracks. Rooftop gardens are very popular, and gardens often go up the sides of tall buildings.

3 City planners have used park areas and water areas to give the city a feeling of space. One of the most **remarkable** parks is the Gardens by the Bay. In addition to plants and flowers, huge artificial "supertrees" have plants in them and collect solar energy. The Gardens by the Bay have had over 40 million visitors. Although Singapore is crowded, its many gardens make it a wonderful city to live in.

CAIRO

4 Being green is a big challenge in the **ancient** city of Cairo, Egypt. With a population of 12 million people, the city is **surrounded** by desert and salt water. When Aga Khan IV visited Cairo in 1984, he saw a busy city that had no large park for residents to enjoy. He wanted to help build a park in the

middle of the city. Finding a location in this ancient city was a major challenge. Finally, they found a place: a 500-year-old trash dump in a poor neighborhood. The Aga Khan gave $30 million (25.5 million euros) to create the park. After removing 80,000 truckloads of dirt and trash, Al-Azhar Park was finished in 2004.

5   Today this park is a sea of green. It has over 650,000 plants, fountains, pools, a lake, open-air theaters, cafes, and restaurants. There are beautiful views of Cairo's historic Old City, with its many famous, ancient mosques. Residents of the Old City are very proud of their neighborhood's history and the park. On the weekends, it is crowded with residents and tourists relaxing and playing in the park.

VANCOUVER

6   The busy seaside city of Vancouver is one of Canada's most densely populated cities. It has a population of over 630,000 and about 2.5 million people in the greater metropolitan area. Although Vancouver is not a huge city, it has big dreams. It is planning on becoming the world's greenest city. In 2011, the city approved a Greenest City Action Plan. One of the goals is to make changes so that all Vancouver residents live within five minutes of a park, greenway, or other green space.

7   One way that Vancouver is adding more nature is by adding trees. Its goal is to **plant** 150,000 trees in ten years. By the end of 2017, it had already planted 102,000 trees. The trees clean the air, give **wildlife** a place to live, and give residents a bit of nature. In addition, there is a program to "rewild" areas of the city. The idea is to return some park areas such as ponds and streams to their wild, natural condition. "Rewilded" areas also educate people about the wildlife that lives there.

8   Perhaps the biggest change over the past ten years has been the increase in bicyclists. There are now over 800 miles of bike lanes in the city. People feel safe riding in the city. As a result, more and more people are bicycling to work and school. Bicyclists say that their daily rides help them feel connected with their communities and help them enjoy nature as they ride.

¹**green city:** a city that supports the protection of the environment

Al-Azhar Park in Cairo, Egypt

B. IDENTIFY What is the main purpose of this article?

☐ 1. To give tourist information about three different cities

☐ 2. To compare how well three cities have used nature

☐ 3. To explain how three cities have increased nature

☐ 4. To show how city residents can enjoy nature around the world

C. RESTATE Complete the chart with notes from the reading. Then compare your notes with a partner.

City	Notes
1. Singapore	
Population	over 5.7 million people
Unique features	an island nation; 100% of people live in urban area
Nature added	huge garden with plants and trees
Interesting fact	over 40 million visitors
2. Cairo	
Population	
Unique features	
Nature added	
Interesting fact	
3. Vancouver	
Population	
Unique features	
Nature added	
Interesting fact	

D. IDENTIFY Find and underline each word in the reading. Read the sentences around the word. Then use the context to guess the correct meaning. Compare your answers with a partner.

1. Paragraph 3: artificial "supertrees"

   a. large trees that are not real

   b. trees that fly

   c. naturally tall trees

2. Paragraph 4: trash

   a. dead plants

   b. recycled bottles

   c. garbage

3. Paragraph 6: densely populated

   a. a large population

   b. people living close together

   c. people from many cultures

4. Paragraph 6: greenway

   a. golf courses

   b. pathways in green areas

   c. sidewalks next to streets

5. Paragraph 7: ponds and streams

   a. large areas of water

   b. small areas of water

   c. very small lakes and small rivers

E. DISCUSS Discuss the questions in a group.

1. How did the government of Singapore help the city become more green?

2. What did the government of Vancouver do in 2011? Why is it important for a city to have a plan for the future?

3. How long was it between when Aga Khan IV visited Cairo and when the Al-Azhar Park opened? Why do you think it took so long to build the park?

4. What city would you be most interested in visiting? Why?

5. How could your city become greener? Which approach from the article might work in your city?

WORK WITH THE VIDEO

A. PREVIEW Discuss the questions with a partner.

1. Do people in your area have gardens? What do they grow?

2. What is your favorite vegetable? Where does it grow?

VIDEO VOCABULARY

road trip (phr.) a trip made in a car over a long distance

lot (n.) an area of land used for a particular purpose

food desert (idiom) a city area where it is difficult to buy fresh food

organic (adj.) produced by or using natural materials, not chemicals

iQ RESOURCES Go online to watch the video about Growing Cities.
Resources > Unit 7 > Unit Video

B. CATEGORIZE Watch the video two or three times. Then write the phrases in the correct category in the chart.

Dan and Andrew are from here	people don't have enough fresh food
first city in the road trip	people used to grow their own food
many empty lots	second city in the road trip
not much empty space	space for gardens on rooftops

Omaha, Nebraska	Detroit, Michigan	New York City, New York

C. DISCUSS Discuss the questions in a group.

1. What ideas from the video would work in your city or town?

2. In a city, most food is shipped in from farms far away. Why is it good to have vegetable gardens in a city?

WRITE WHAT YOU THINK

SYNTHESIZE Think about Reading 1, Reading 2, and the unit video as you discuss the question. Then write a response.

Do you think adding vegetable gardens to parks would be good for your city? Why?

VOCABULARY SKILL Phrasal Verbs

A phrasal verb is a *verb* + a *particle*. Some examples of particles are *in, out, up, over, by, down,* and *away.* When a particle is added to a verb, it often creates a new meaning.

> I want to **watch** the game on TV tonight. (watch = look at)
> **Watch out** for ice on the stairs! (watch out = be careful)

Many phrasal verbs have more than one meaning.

> He **picked up** the book and started to read. (lifted)
> Abdullah **picked up** his friend in his new red car. (gave a ride to)
> The wind **picked up** in the afternoon. (increased)

Some phrasal verbs are separable. They can be separated by objects.

> He **picked up** the book.   Yolanda **threw away** her old shoes.
> He **picked** the book **up**.   Yolanda **threw** her old shoes **away**.

Some phrasal verbs are inseparable. They cannot be separated by an object.

> ✓ The passengers got on the train.   ✓ Eva stopped by my house yesterday.
> ✗ The passengers got the train on.   ✗ Eva stopped my house by yesterday.

A. APPLY Read the sentences. Then circle the answer that best matches the meaning of each bold phrasal verb.

1. We are hoping to **get away** to the mountains in the summer.

   a. return

   b. take a vacation

2. The printer was very cheap, so it wasn't surprising that it **fell apart**.

   a. broke into pieces

   b. got old

3. The city **ran out of** money before they finished the new highway.

   a. get more of

   b. finish a supply of

4. Paulo **wore out** his favorite jeans, so he had to buy another pair.

   a. repaired

   b. used too much

5. The students like to **get together** in the plaza between classes.

   a. meet socially

   b. have lunch

B. APPLY Rewrite the sentences putting the object between the verb and the particle.

1. The parents picked up the children from school.

   The parents picked the children up from school.

2. Please throw away your trash. Don't leave it on the desk.

   _____

3. Put on your hat. It's very cold outside!

   _____

4. I usually clean up the kitchen after dinner.

   _____

5. I walk a lot, so I wear out my shoes quickly.

   _____

iQ PRACTICE Go online for more practice with phrasal verbs.
Practice > Unit 7 > Activity 8

WRITING

OBJECTIVE ▶ At the end of this unit, you will write a paragraph about nature in your town or city. Your paragraph will include specific information from the readings and your own ideas.

GRAMMAR Simple past and past continuous

Use the **simple past** to describe a single completed action or a series of completed actions in the past.

- I **bought** the new novel by my favorite author yesterday.
- Mark **drove** home, **unloaded** his car, and **made** a cup of coffee.

Also use the simple past to describe a habitual or repeated action in the past.

- Last summer, I **went** to the park every weekend.
- I **sent** Leila three emails, but she never **replied**.

Use the **past continuous** to emphasize the duration of an action in the past.

- I **was talking** on the phone for hours last night.
- My brother **was acting** strangely yesterday.

If a past event was interrupted by another event or series of events, use *while* or *when* with the past continuous for the interrupted event. Use the simple past for the event or events that interrupted it.

- Sultan **left** the room <u>while</u> the teacher **was** still **talking**.
- <u>When</u> I **was studying** in South Korea, I **met** many interesting people.

A. IDENTIFY Read the sentences. Check (✓) the function of the simple past (in bold) in the sentence.

	single action	series of actions	repeated action
1. I **left** the restaurant at 6:00 p.m. last night.	☐	☐	☐
2. When the president **came** into the room, everyone **stood up** and **clapped**.	☐	☐	☐
3. Eric **rewrote** his story five times.	☐	☐	☐
4. My friend **visited** me every day while I **was** sick.	☐	☐	☐
5. Someone **stole** my bike last week.	☐	☐	☐
6. Jessica **finished** her letter, **put** it in an envelope, and **took** it to the post office.	☐	☐	☐

B. IDENTIFY Read the sentences. Check (✓) the function of the past continuous (in bold) in the sentence.

	duration	interrupted action
1. Jim broke his leg while he **was playing** soccer.	☐	☐
2. I **was watching** TV all weekend.	☐	☐
3. When Natalia **was working** in the science lab, she discovered a mistake.	☐	☐
4. You **were complaining** the whole time at the restaurant last night.	☐	☐

iQ PRACTICE Go online for more practice with simple past and past continuous. *Practice ⟩ Unit 7 ⟩ Activities 9–10*

WRITING SKILL Using sentence variety

Using different types of sentences will make your writing more interesting. Here are some ways to improve your sentence variety.

1. Use both long and short sentences.
2. If you have too many short sentences, combine two sentences into one compound sentence with a coordinating conjunction (*and*, *but,* or *so*).

   The city wanted to plant more trees. They approved a ten-year plan.

   The city wanted to plant more trees, <u>so</u> they approved a ten-year plan.
3. Use questions and imperatives.

Look at these examples from Reading 2.

People feel safe riding in the city. As a result, more and more people are bicycling to work and school.

Rooftop gardens are very popular, and gardens often go up the sides of tall buildings.

Can every city become a green city? Read and decide for yourself.

A. IDENTIFY Read the paragraph. Then answer the questions. Compare your answers with a partner.

^{1} Was New York City's Central Park always as beautiful as it is today? ^{2} Unfortunately, it was not. ^{3} Today it is a peaceful park, but it was not always a clean or safe place. ^{4} When it was first created in 1857, it became one of the first large public parks in the United States. ^{5} In the 1900s, there wasn't money to repair the park, so no one took care of the trees and buildings. ^{6} By the 1970s, no one wanted to visit the park. ^{7} It was too unsafe. ^{8} In the late 1970s, a new management company came in, and slowly the park was repaired. ^{9} Central Park became a beautiful and safe place again, so people could once again enjoy the park. ^{10} Nowadays, the park is enjoyed by residents and tourists, and it offers people a bit of peace in the middle of New York City. ^{11} Be sure to visit Central Park.

1. What sentences are short? _____

2. What sentences have coordinating conjunctions? Underline the conjunctions.
   _____

3. What sentence is a question? _____

4. What sentence is an imperative? _____

B. RESTATE Combine the two short sentences into one sentence. Use *and*, *but*, or *so*.

1. Istanbul, Turkey, has over 15 million residents. Istanbul is the country's largest city.

   _____

2. Istanbul has many ancient historic sites. Tourists enjoy modern attractions as well.

   _____

3. Turkey is between Europe and Asia. Turkey shares features of many cultures.

   _____

4. Istanbul is the largest city. Ankara is the capital.

   _____

5. Turkey has 40 national parks. It has 189 nature parks.

   _____

C. CREATE Finish each sentence in your own words.

1. Our city park is _____, so

_____.

2. People who ride bicycles in a city _____,

and they _____.

3. In my opinion, trees in a city _____.

4. Why should _____?

5. Don't _____.

iQ PRACTICE Go online for more practice with using sentence variety.
Practice > Unit 7 > Activity 11

UNIT ASSIGNMENT Write an opinion paragraph

OBJECTIVE ▶

In this assignment, you will write an opinion paragraph about nature in your town or city. As you prepare to write, think about the Unit Question, "Do cities need nature?" Use information from Reading 1, Reading 2, the unit video, and your work in this unit to support your paragraph. Refer to the Self-Assessment checklist on page 168.

iQ PRACTICE Go online to the Writing Tutor to read a model opinion paragraph. *Practice > Unit 7 > Activity 13*

PLAN AND WRITE

CRITICAL THINKING STRATEGY

Analyzing and evaluating ideas

One way to **analyze and evaluate** your ideas before you write is to ask yourself questions. For example, if you are going to write an opinion paragraph, write your opinion or main idea at the top of your paper. Then ask yourself questions to analyze and evaluate your opinion. For example:

Is my opinion important to discuss? Why?

Is my opinion a statement that I can support with reasons? Do I have at least three reasons for support?

Do I have facts and examples to support each reason?

Will my reasons convince the reader to agree with my opinion?

Read the student notes for an opinion paragraph.

Opinion: We don't need more trees along our city streets. (This is important to discuss because the city is preparing to spend thousands of dollars to plant new trees along certain city streets.)

Reason 1: We already have many trees, especially along downtown streets. (Give the approximate number of trees.)

Reason 2: Old trees can fall and injure people. (Include stories about several injuries last year.)

Reason 3: Trees are more important in parks. (Describe a park that needs more trees, and explain why they are important.)

iQ PRACTICE Go online to watch the Critical Thinking Video and check your comprehension. *Practice > Unit 7 > Activity 12*

A. **DISCUSS** What is your opinion about nature in your city? Is there enough nature? Should there be more nature? Is there too much nature? Discuss these questions with a partner.

B. **PLAN** Decide on the opinion you will write about. Ask yourself the following questions to analyze and evaluate your ideas. Then complete the rough outline for your paragraph.

Is my opinion important to discuss? Why?

Is my opinion a statement that I can support with reasons? Do I have at least three reasons for support?

Do I have facts and examples to support each reason?

Will my reasons convince the reader to agree with my opinion?

Opinion: _____

This is important because: _____

_____

Reason 1: _____

Facts or examples: _____

Reason 2: _____

Facts or examples: _____

Reason 3: _____

Facts or examples: _____

iQ RESOURCES Go online to download and complete the outline for your opinion paragraph. *Resources > Writing Tools > Unit 7 > Outline*

C. WRITE Use your rough outline from Activity B to write your paragraph.

1. Write a clear topic sentence and use reasons and details to support your opinion. Make sure to use a variety of sentences. Be sure you have a concluding sentence. Try to use some expressions for giving opinions, some phrasal verbs, and the simple past or past continuous.

2. Look at the Self-Assessment checklist below to guide your writing.

iQ PRACTICE Go online to the Writing Tutor to write your assignment.
Practice › Unit 7 › Activity 14

REVISE AND EDIT

iQ RESOURCES Go online to download the peer review worksheet.
Resource › Unit 7 › Peer Review

A. PEER REVIEW Read your partner's paragraph. Then use the peer review worksheet. Discuss the review with your partner.

B. REWRITE Based on your partner's review, revise and rewrite your paragraph.

C. EDIT Complete the Self-Assessment checklist as you prepare to write the final draft of your paragraph. Be prepared to hand in your work or discuss it in class.

SELF-ASSESSMENT	Yes	No
Do you make claims? Are they supported by facts?	☐	☐
Do you use simple past and past continuous correctly?	☐	☐
Do you have a variety of sentences?	☐	☐
Does your paragraph include vocabulary from the unit?	☐	☐
Did you check the paragraph for punctuation, spelling, and grammar?	☐	☐

D. REFLECT Discuss these questions with a partner or group.

1. What is something new you learned in this unit?

2. Look back at the Unit Question—Do cities need nature? Is your answer different now than when you started the unit? If yes, how is it different? Why?

iQ PRACTICE Go to the online discussion board to discuss the questions.
Practice › Unit 7 › Activity 15

TRACK YOUR SUCCESS

iQ PRACTICE   Go online to check the words and phrases you have learned in this unit. *Practice > Unit 7 > Activity 16*

Check (✓) the skills and strategies you learned. If you need more work on a skill, refer to the page(s) in parentheses.

READING	☐ I can identify claims and support. (p. 152)
VOCABULARY	☐ I can use phrasal verbs. (p. 161)
GRAMMAR	☐ I can use the simple past and past continuous. (p. 163)
WRITING	☐ I can use a variety of sentences. (p. 164)
CRITICAL THINKING	☐ I can analyze and evaluate ideas. (p. 166)

OBJECTIVE ▶   ☐ I can gather information and ideas to write an opinion paragraph about nature in a city.

Public
Health

8

READING	synthesizing information
CRITICAL THINKING	summarizing main ideas
VOCABULARY	collocations
WRITING	writing an explanatory paragraph
GRAMMAR	adverbs of manner and degree

How can we prevent diseases?

A. Discuss these questions with your classmates.

1. When was the last time you were sick? How did you feel? How did you get sick?

2. What are some things you do to avoid getting sick?

3. Look at the photo. Why is the boy wearing a mask?

B. Listen to *The Q Classroom* online. Then answer these questions.

1. What six ways to prevent disease did the speakers mention? Fill in the chart below. Then for each one, check (✓) how often you do it. When you finish, discuss your chart with your classmates.

2. Do you agree with Sophy and Felix that people should wear face masks or stay home when they are sick? Why or why not?

iQ PRACTICE Go to the online discussion board to discuss the Unit Question with your classmates. *Practice > Unit 8 > Activity 1*

Ways to prevent diseases		Always	Sometimes	Rarely	Never
a.	*eat right*				
b.					
c.					
d.					
e.					
f.					

UNIT OBJECTIVE

Read the articles. Gather information and ideas to write an explanatory paragraph about an illness.

READING

READING 1

University Health Center: Cold News

OBJECTIVE ▶

You are going to read a web page from a university health website. Use the web page to gather information and ideas for your Unit Assignment.

PREVIEW THE READING

A. VOCABULARY Here are some words from Reading 1. Read the sentences. Then write each underlined word or phrase next to the correct definition.

1. You should <u>cover</u> your baby with extra blankets in the winter, so he doesn't get cold.

2. Finding a <u>cure</u> for cancer is very important.

3. I hope my cold doesn't <u>develop</u> into a bad cough. It's already worse than it was yesterday.

4. Colds are <u>extremely</u> common among schoolchildren during winter. Both of my children have colds right now.

5. The child had a high <u>fever</u>, so the father took her to the doctor.

6. If you have a cold and you sneeze on other people, you can <u>infect</u> them.

7. Your overall health is directly <u>related to</u> how well you eat and how often you exercise.

8. Pria had a <u>severe</u> pain in her back, so I took her to the hospital.

9. A sore throat is a common <u>symptom</u> of a cold.

10. A <u>virus</u> causes the common cold. It spreads from person to person quickly.

a. _____ (*adjective phrase*) connected with something

b. _____ (*noun*) something that shows that you have an illness

c. _____ (*noun*) a living thing that is too small to see but that makes you sick

d. _____ (*verb*) to put something on or in front of something else to protect it

e. _____ (*verb*) to give a disease to someone

f. _____ (*adjective*) very bad

g. _____ (*adverb*) very

h. _____ (*verb*) to grow slowly, increase, or change into something else

i. _____ (*noun*) a medicine or medical treatment that will make an illness go away

j. _____ (*noun*) a temperature that is higher than normal

iQ PRACTICE   Go online for more practice with the vocabulary.
Practice > Unit 8 > Activities 2–3

B. PREVIEW This web page is from a university health center website. Read the questions in the headings. Which ones can you answer without reading the answers?

C. QUICK WRITE Think about the last time you had a bad cold. Write your responses to the questions before you read the web page. Be sure to use this section for your Unit Assignment.

1. What were your symptoms?

2. How long were you sick? Did you stay home from school or work?

3. What helped you feel better while you were sick?

WORK WITH THE READING

 A. INVESTIGATE Read the web page and gather information about colds on college campuses.

UNIVERSITY HEALTH CENTER: COLD NEWS

1   *Kenji just finished a week of exams. In the weeks before the exams, he stayed up late, ate poorly, and felt stressed. After he finished his exams, he wanted to relax with his friends. But he felt **extremely** tired and sick. He had **developed** a terrible cold, so he went back to bed.*

2   Kenji has had a typical college experience: a bad cold that sends him to bed and slows him down for a week or so. Doctors say that college students have an average of four to six colds a year, more than the average adult, who has about two colds per year. According to health experts, college students have more colds and diseases than other students.

WHY DO COLLEGE STUDENTS GET MORE COLDS?

3   First, college students live, eat, and study very close together on a college campus. First year students often attend large classes with 200 students crowded into one big classroom. In addition, students often share cups, glasses, spoons, and forks. So, there are many opportunities for germs[1] to spread. Second, college students are under a lot of academic and social stress. Stress makes it harder for the body to fight disease. Finally, the lifestyle of a college student often means poor sleep, smoking, too much fast food, and other unhealthy habits. For these reasons, college students have more colds than other people.

WHAT ARE SYMPTOMS OF A COLD?

4   A cold usually starts with **symptoms** such as a sore throat, a headache, and low energy. Then the runny nose[2] starts. You may also have a cough. A cold can last a few days or a few weeks. Every cold is different because colds are caused by over 200 different **viruses**. Unlike a cold, the flu (influenza) is more **severe**, begins very suddenly, and causes a **fever**.

WHY CAN'T I TAKE AN ANTIBIOTIC[3] FOR A COLD?

5   Currently, there is no **cure** for the common cold. Antibiotics will not help you feel better if you have a cold. Antibiotics only cure bacterial infections[4], and a cold is caused by a virus. There are some medications that may help you feel better, but they will not make a cold go away.

WHY ARE COLDS MORE COMMON IN COLD WEATHER?

6   Cold weather is usually dry, and dry air makes it easier for viruses to spread. Viruses are found indoors, and that is where people stay during cold weather. Colds are also common in the spring and summer.

HOW CAN I AVOID GETTING A COLD?

7   First of all, your health is directly **related to** how well you take care of yourself. Get enough sleep, eat well, and make time to relax. Second, avoid people who have a cold. The cold virus spreads in little drops of moisture[5] in the air. When someone coughs or sneezes, he or she can spread a virus. Finally, wash your hands frequently. Virus germs can stay on a doorknob, computer keyboard, or table for up to 48 hours.

HOW CAN I AVOID SPREADING A COLD TO OTHERS?

8   The most important thing is to stay away from others and rest. It's also very important to **cover** your mouth with your elbow or a tissue when you sneeze. Wash your hands often because viruses are most often carried on your fingers. You can also wear a face mask, which prevents some of the virus droplets from traveling to others.

WHAT ELSE CAN I DO TO PREVENT THE SPREAD OF COLD VIRUSES OR OTHER INFECTIOUS DISEASES?

9
- Clean surfaces of things that are used often, such as desks, doorknobs, and cell phones.
- Don't get too close to others who are sick.
- Do not share food, glasses, cups, or knives, forks, and spoons. Also, do not share towels.
- Don't travel when you are sick. You may **infect** others who are sitting close by.

10   Getting a cold is common for college students, but you can take steps to stay healthy. If you do catch a cold, the best thing is to rest and avoid spreading it to others.

[1]**germs:** very small living things that cause diseases
[2]**runny nose:** used to describe the condition when a sticky liquid substance flows from your nose because of a cold
[3]**antibiotic:** a medicine that is used for destroying bacteria and curing infections
[4]**bacterial infections:** diseases or illnesses caused by very small living things
[5]**moisture:** water in small drops on a surface or in the air

B. CATEGORIZE Read the statements. Then check (✓) main idea or supporting detail.

	Main idea	Supporting detail
1. College students get more colds than adults.		
2. Students often share cups and glasses.		
3. A cold can last a few days or a few weeks.		
4. Antibiotics don't cure colds.		
5. Viruses are found indoors.		
6. Students need to get enough sleep.		
7. Virus germs can stay on a doorknob for up to 48 hours.		
8. College students can make changes to stay healthy.		

C. IDENTIFY Correct these false statements with information from Reading 1. Write the paragraph number where the answer is found.

1. College students have an average of two to four colds per year.

   Paragraph: ____ _____

2. College students get more colds because they live, eat, and study at home.

   Paragraph: ____ _____

3. Colds are caused by several different types of viruses.

   Paragraph: ____ _____

4. A cold is similar to the flu (influenza).

   Paragraph: ____ _____

5. People get more colds during cold weather because viruses spread easily in humid air.

   Paragraph: ____ _____

6. A sneeze or a cough cannot spread virus germs.

   Paragraph: ____ _____

7. The article suggests that students can share food safely.

   Paragraph: ____ _____

8. The best thing to do when you catch a cold is to take antibiotics.

   Paragraph: ____ _____

D. EXTEND Look back at the reading on pages 173–174 and answer these questions. Then discuss your answers in a group.

1. What is an additional question to add to the university health center web page? Why would this be a good question to add?

_____

_____

2. What do you think the answer might be?

_____

_____

iQ PRACTICE   Go online for additional reading and comprehension.
Practice > Unit 8 > Activity 4

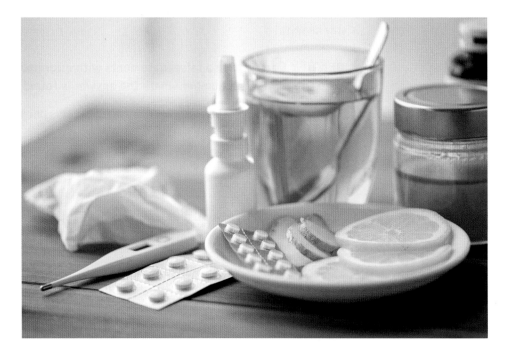

 # WRITE WHAT YOU THINK

A. DISCUSS Discuss these questions in a group.

1. The reading gives tips on how to avoid getting a cold. What are some other things you can do?

2. Some people worry a lot about catching a cold from others, and some people are not very concerned. How concerned are you, on a scale from 1 to 10 (10 = extremely concerned, 1 = not concerned at all)? Explain your answers.

3. What other illnesses or diseases are you interested in learning more about? What do you want to know about them?

B. SYNTHESIZE Choose one of the questions and write a response. Look back at your Quick Write on page 173 as you think about what you learned.

Question: _____

My Response: _____

_____

_____

READING SKILL Synthesizing information

When you **synthesize** information, you develop a new understanding about a topic by using information from more than one source. For example, you can synthesize information from two different readings to answer a question. You can also synthesize what you already know about a topic and the new information you are learning about that topic from an article you are reading.

Reading 1
Reading 2
What I already know
Newspaper article
→ **Synthesizing information** → Deeper understanding

Synthesizing information helps you deepen and expand your knowledge. It is also important because some test questions and writing assignments ask you to synthesize information you have read.

A. IDENTIFY Answer these questions.

1. Think back to Reading 1. What information in the reading was new to you? What information did you already know?

   _____

   _____

2. Read these questions about Reading 1. Which one is a **synthesis** question? Which is a **main idea** question? Which is a **detail** question? Label each one.

   a. _____ How do colds spread?

   b. _____ After reading this web page, will you change any of your health habits? Why or why not?

   c. _____ What is the difference between the flu and a cold?

3. Answer the questions in item 2. For the synthesis question, be sure to use information that you already know and information from the reading.

a. _____

b. _____

c. _____

B. SYNTHESIZE Read this paragraph. Then answer the synthesis questions, using what you already know, information in the paragraph, and the information in Reading 1.

> Just like humans, animals get flu viruses, too. These animal viruses rarely spread to humans, but occasionally they do. For example, an avian flu, also called bird flu, can spread from birds to humans. Once a person gets a virus from an animal, it then spreads very quickly from person to person, just like other types of the flu. Flu viruses that come from animals can be dangerous to humans and can make people extremely sick. People do not have natural protection for these new viruses, and it can take a very long time for medicines to be developed. There is often an increased possibility of death with illnesses like avian flu.

1. Is the avian flu more dangerous than the seasonal flu? Explain your answer.

_____

_____

2. How do you think an avian flu can spread from an animal to a human? How does it spread to many people?

_____

_____

iQ PRACTICE Go online for more practice with synthesizing information. *Practice > Unit 8 > Activity 5*

READING 2 Preventing Disease Around the World

OBJECTIVE ▶

You are going to read a magazine article about doctors' efforts to prevent the spread of disease in different parts of the world. Use the article to gather information and ideas for your Unit Assignment.

PREVIEW THE READING

VOCABULARY SKILL REVIEW

In Unit 7, you learned about phrasal verbs. Find the two phrasal verbs in paragraph 2 and paragraph 8 of Reading 1 (*slow down* and *stay away*). Using a dictionary, find out if these phrasal verbs are separable or inseparable.

A. VOCABULARY Here are some words from Reading 2. Read their definitions. Then complete each sentence.

contagious *(adjective)* used about a disease that you can get by touching someone or something

contaminated *(adjective)* containing something dirty, harmful, or dangerous

emergency *(noun)* 🔑 a serious event or situation that needs immediate action

outbreak *(noun)* the sudden start of something bad, such as a disease

prevention *(noun)* the act of stopping something from happening

risk *(noun)* the possibility of something bad happening in the future

source *(noun)* 🔑 OPAL a place where something comes from or is obtained

take steps (to do) *(verb phrase)* to take action in order to achieve something

treat *(verb)* to give medical care or attention to a person, an illness, or an injury

volunteer *(verb)* OPAL to agree to do something that you don't have to do or that you will not be paid for

🔑 Oxford 3000™ words   OPAL Oxford Phrasal Academic Lexicon

1. No one wanted to do the job until Jenny said she would _____.

2. If you break a bone, have a doctor _____ you immediately.

3. The explorers followed the river all the way to its _____.

4. People who smoke cigarettes _____ getting lung cancer.

5. Get out of the way! Let the police car get to the _____.

6. Don't drink that water! It is _____!

7. Take care of yourself. _____ is better than getting sick.

8. In the elementary school, there was an _____ of the flu. About 30 percent of the kids got sick.

9. Don't get too close to me or you might catch my cold. It is very _____.

10. The doctors knew that they had to _____ immediately to prevent the disease from spreading.

PRACTICE Go online for more practice with the vocabulary.
Practice ⟩ Unit 8 ⟩ Activities 6–7

WORK WITH THE READING

A. INVESTIGATE Read the magazine article and gather information about how we can prevent diseases.

PREVENTING DISEASE AROUND THE WORLD

Dr. Jean Andersson-Swayze at work

1   Jean Andersson-Swayze is on vacation. Well, not exactly vacation. Jean is a doctor, and she is taking time away from her usual work in the United States to take care of people in Haiti who are sick. Jean is part of a group of health-care workers who try to help stop disease and help people live healthier lives around the world. She has worked with refugees[1] in Greece, and she has made a number of trips to Haiti, including one after a bad earthquake.

2   In 2015, a terrible virus called Ebola began to kill people in West Africa. Dr. Andersson-Swayze **volunteered** with the International Medical Corps to help **treat** the **outbreak**. The disease was extremely **contagious**—it spread very quickly—and she needed to wear a special suit to avoid catching the illness. Even though the doctor and others worked very hard to save them, many people died from the disease. Fortunately, the Ebola outbreak in West Africa is no longer an **emergency**.

3   In addition to taking care of people who are already sick, the doctor is a strong believer in the **prevention** of disease. One of the most common reasons that people are sick around the world is because they do not have enough water or do not have clean water.

Without any water at all, people can die from dehydration. That is, their bodies don't have enough water to keep them alive. Other people in the world do have water, but it is not clean.

4   People who drink water that is not clean are at **risk** of getting sick. More than 800,000 people die each year as a result of unsafe drinking water. The water may be **contaminated** by chemicals or human waste. More than 2 billion people do not have clean running water in their homes. Often, they must travel long distances every day to get to a dependable **source** of clean water to drink. Helping people get a supply of clean water can prevent many diseases and loss of life.

5   Another helpful organization is called Pure Water for the World. This group and others help set up better access to clean drinking

water. They work closely with local people and educate residents about the importance of clean water. It is essential not only to help people get clean water, but also to be sure that they know how to keep the water clean.

6   In the same way that Dr. Andersson-Swayze is helping, others are also trying to stop disease. Many diseases are spread by insects, especially mosquitoes. In 2016, 445,000 people died from malaria, a disease that is spread by insects. If the disease is found early, it can be treated with drugs. But there is an easy way to **take steps** to prevent the disease: mosquito netting. A mosquito net is like a thin curtain that you use to cover your bed when you go to sleep. If the mosquitoes can't bite you, then they can't infect you with malaria. This is a very simple and inexpensive solution to a deadly problem.

7   The Bill and Melinda Gates Foundation is one group that is trying to fight malaria. Bill Gates, the founder of Microsoft, is contributing millions of dollars to help improve public health. The focus of this organization is on managing infectious diseases[2] and developing cures for the diseases that cause children to die when they are very young.

8   In many parts of the world, poor public health is a severe problem. Some people such as Dr. Andersson-Swayze are trying to help people one by one. Organizations like Pure Water for the World and the Gates Foundation are looking at larger solutions. Perhaps together they can help solve these global issues.

Mosquito netting helps stop the spread of malaria

[1]**refugees:** people who must leave their country because of war or other problems
[2]**infectious diseases:** illnesses that can be spread quickly and easily

B. **EXPLAIN** Answer the questions. Write the paragraph number(s) where the answer is found.

1. In what parts of the world has Dr. Andersson-Swayze worked?

   Paragraph: ____ _____

2. Why did she have to wear a special suit while treating Ebola?

   Paragraph: ____ _____

3. What is a common reason that people get sick around the world?

   Paragraph: ____ _____

4. How many people don't have clean running water in their homes?

   Paragraph: ____ _____

5. What insect spreads malaria?

   Paragraph: ____ _____

6. What is an easy way to prevent the spread of malaria?

   Paragraph: ____ _____

C. CATEGORIZE Read the statements. Write *T* (true) or *F* (false). Then correct each false statement to make it true. Write the paragraph number where the answer is found.

1. Dr. Andersson-Swayze usually works in Canada.

   Paragraph: ____ _____

2. Ebola is not a very dangerous disease.

   Paragraph: ____ _____

3. It is important not only to treat diseases but to prevent them.

   Paragraph: ____ _____

4. Unclean water is usually contaminated by too much salt.

   Paragraph: ____ _____

5. Education is an important part of helping people keep their water clean.

   Paragraph: ____ _____

6. If it is found early, malaria can be treated with drugs.

   Paragraph: ____ _____

7. The Gates Foundation has given hundreds of dollars to help improve public health.

   Paragraph: ____ _____

8. Poor public health is a problem in many parts of the world.

   Paragraph: ____ _____

D. APPLY Complete the paragraphs below with details from the reading.

In many parts of the world _____ public health is a problem. Some
1
doctors travel around the world to help take _____ of people who are sick. In
2
Africa, there was an _____ of the Ebola virus. Many people died. A _____
3 4
reason why people get sick is that they do not have enough _____ or clean
5
_____. Without water, people can die from _____.
6 7

Another disease that kills many people is _____. This disease is spread by
8
insects called _____. However, an inexpensive way to prevent malaria is by
9
using mosquito _____. Doctors hope to solve the problems of public health
10
around the world.

E. IDENTIFY What is the author's purpose in this reading? More than one answer is possible.

a. to tell an interesting story

b. to make the reader laugh

c. to make the reader excited about the topic

d. to give information

e. to explain a situation

 CRITICAL THINKING STRATEGY

Summarizing main ideas

When you **summarize**, you write a short version of what you read. You only include the most important points, not all of the small details. Writing a summary helps you see "the big picture," or the main message, of a text.

Look back at Paragraph 1 on page 180, which has five sentences. If we summarize the paragraph in one sentence, we could write:

> Dr. Jean Andersson-Swayze travels around the world treating sick people, so they become well again.

Notice that the summary does not contain all of the details. It leaves out many of the points. For example, it doesn't say what countries she has visited. But that's OK. A summary is just the short version. We don't want all of those details.

iQ PRACTICE Go online to watch the Critical Thinking Video and check your comprehension. *Practice > Unit 8 > Activity 8*

F. IDENTIFY Look at Paragraph 2 on page 180. Check (✓) the best summary.

☐ 1. Dr. Andersson-Swayze had to wear a special suit to avoid the disease.

☐ 2. The outbreak of the Ebola virus killed many people in West Africa.

☐ 3. The disease was very contagious.

G. APPLY Read the paragraphs on pages 180–181. Write a two-sentence summary.

1. Paragraph 3 _____

_____

2. Paragraph 4 _____

_____

3. Paragraph 6 _____

_____

WORK WITH THE VIDEO

A. PREVIEW Vote *yes* or *no* on the following question: Can you catch a cold from being outside in cold weather?

VIDEO VOCABULARY

fact or fiction (expression) true or not

illness (n.) sickness, disease, the state of being not well

key (adj.) very important

peak (adj.) the highest point on a mountain

iQ RESOURCES   Go online to watch the video about science experiments.
Resources › Video › Unit 8 › Unit Video

B. CATEGORIZE Watch the video two or three times. Then answer the questions below for each of the two experiments.

	Javid's experiment	Helen's experiment
What question were they trying to answer?		
What did they do?		
What was the result?		

C. EXTEND Can you think of any other important ways to stay healthy that are not mentioned in the video? What are they?

WRITE WHAT YOU THINK

SYNTHESIZE Think about Reading 1, Reading 2, and the unit video as you discuss these questions. Then choose one question and write a response.

1. Would you be willing to travel to another country to help people who are sick? Where would you go? What would you do?

2. People like doctors can try to help fight disease around the world. They are individuals. Organizations and governments can also help. Do you think it is better for individuals or organizations to try to improve public health? Why?

VOCABULARY SKILL Collocations

ACADEMIC LANGUAGE

The phrase *in response to* is common in academic writing. *The researchers published their raw data in response to criticism of their methods.*

_____ OPAL

Oxford Phrasal Academic Lexicon

A **collocation** is a group of words that frequently go together. Some collocations are made up of a verb + a preposition. Here are some common collocations with the prepositions *on*, *to*, and *in*.

comment on: to give an opinion about something

contribute to: to give a part to the total of something

in common: like or similar to somebody or something

increase in: a rise in the number, amount, or level of something

in favor of: in agreement with someone or something

in response to: an answer or reaction to something

participate in: to share or join in

succeed in: to manage to achieve what you want; to do well

Using collocations will help your speaking and writing sound more natural.

A. APPLY Complete each sentence below with the correct collocation.

comment on	in common	in favor of	participate in
contribute to	increase in	in response to	succeed in

1. A cold and the flu have some things _____. For example, they can both be passed from one person to another.

2. My mother told me she liked my new dress, but she didn't _____ my new haircut. Maybe she doesn't like it.

3. The scientists need 50 people to _____ a scientific study. They will pay each person $500.

4. There's been a(n) _____ cases of malaria this summer. More people are getting sick than last year.

5. Eating lots of green vegetables can _____ your overall health.

6. Sofia nodded her head _____ my question.

7. If you want to _____ becoming an Olympic athlete, you have to train very hard.

8. Keiko was not _____ the new proposal, so she voted against it.

B. COMPOSE Choose five collocations from Activity A. Write a sentence using each one. Then share your sentences with a group.

_____

_____

_____

_____

_____

iQ PRACTICE Go online for more practice with collocations.
Practice ⟩ Unit 8 ⟩ Activity 9

WRITING

OBJECTIVE ▶

At the end of this unit, you will write an explanatory paragraph about an illness. This can include specific information from the readings and your own ideas.

WRITING SKILL Writing an explanatory paragraph

An **explanatory paragraph** defines and explains a term or concept. Use an explanatory paragraph when you want to explain a term or concept that your reader might not know.

Use these guidelines to make your explanatory paragraph clear to your reader.

- First, write a topic sentence that states and defines the term or concept.
- Make sure the definition is clear. Use a dictionary or online sources.
- Then write about the term or concept using explanations and examples.
- Explain how the term or concept is different from similar terms.
- Explain what the term or concept is not.

You can use these sentence structures to write a topic sentence for an explanatory paragraph.

_____ is a _____ that _____.
An <u>inhaler</u> is a <u>device</u> that <u>helps a person with asthma breathe</u>.
_____ is when _____.
An <u>epidemic</u> is when <u>many people have an illness at the same time</u>.

A. IDENTIFY Read the model explanatory paragraph. Then answer the questions on page 188.

An epidemic is when a large number of people have the same disease at the same time. Some diseases are very serious, and they can spread quickly, becoming a public health emergency. An epidemic can also spread to other countries. For example, in 2015 an outbreak of the Zika virus began in Brazil and spread to other countries in South and North America. It was estimated that 1.5 million people were infected with Zika in Brazil. If a woman with Zika has a baby, the child may be born with severe problems in its brain. An epidemic is not the same as a plague, which is a disease that spreads quickly and kills many people. An epidemic sometimes can kill many people, but it doesn't always. However, an epidemic is a serious public health emergency.

1. What is the definition of *epidemic*?

_____

2. What example of an epidemic does the writer give?

_____

3. What does the writer say an epidemic is different from?

_____

4. Compare the paragraph on page 187 with paragraph 4 in Reading 1 on page 174. How are the paragraphs similar? How are they different?

_____

B. **COMPOSE** Write a topic sentence for an explanatory paragraph for each of these topics. Use the two different sentence structures in the skill box on page 187. You may also need to look in the dictionary.

1. A common cold

_____

2. Influenza

_____

3. Ebola

_____

4. Malaria

_____

C. **APPLY** Complete each of the sentences related to the four topics in Activity B. The sentences will help explain your topic by saying what it is NOT or by using contrast.

1. _A cold_____ is not the same as the flu, _which is_____ a more severe illness.

2. Although a(n) _____ is similar to the flu, flu symptoms are more _____.

3. Like a(n) _____, a cluster is the spread of an infectious disease. However, in a(n) _____, the number of people affected is much smaller.

4. Ebola is a highly _____ disease. It is not like heart disease, which _____ be spread from one person to another.

5. Some _____ can be spread by human contact, but malaria is spread _____.

WRITING TIP
In Activity D, you will complete an idea map to brainstorm ideas. Brainstorming ideas in this way will result in better writing.

D. IDENTIFY Choose one of the topics in Activity B and complete the idea map to plan your writing. For examples, you can list symptoms or characteristics, depending on your topic.

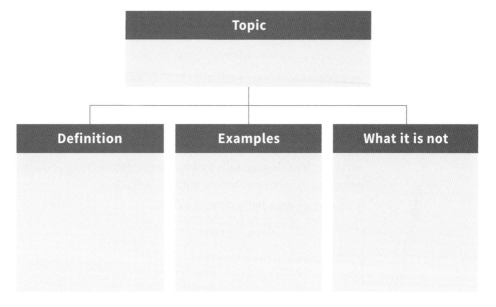

E. COMPOSE Write your explanatory paragraph. Use the guidelines in the Writing Skill box, topics from Activity B, and your idea map in Activity D.

F. ANALYZE Share your paragraph with another student who wrote about the same topic. Compare your paragraphs. Discuss these questions.

1. How are your topic sentences different? Which topic sentence is stronger? Why?

_____

2. How many examples are in each of your paragraphs? Which examples are similar?

_____

3. Compare each other's sentences that say what your topic is not. How are they different? How do you think this information helps the reader?

_____

G. CREATE Work together with your partner to write a new explanatory paragraph. Use the best parts of each of your paragraphs.

iQ PRACTICE   Go online for more practice with explanatory paragraphs.
Practice > Unit 8 > Activity 10

GRAMMAR Adverbs of manner and degree

An **adverb of manner** describes how something is done or how something happens. It usually comes after the verb or object.

> Our team played **hard** and won the game **easily**.
> verb   adverb   verb   object   adverb

In sentences with an auxiliary verb, *-ly* adverbs of manner can come between the auxiliary verb and the main verb.

> His temperature was **rapidly** rising during the afternoon.
> auxiliary   adverb   verb

An **adverb of degree** tells to what degree something is done or happens. It comes before an adjective or before another adverb.

> It was an **especially** difficult exam.
> adverb   adjective

> The man was breathing **fairly** slowly.
> adverb   adverb

Here are some common adverbs of degree:

lesser degree   **greater degree**

⟵──⟶

hardly   somewhat   pretty   quite   fairly   so   really   very   especially   extremely

iQ RESOURCES   Go online to watch the Grammar Skill Video.
Resources > Video > Unit 8 > Grammar Skill Video

A. IDENTIFY Write the adverb form of each of the adjectives below. Then complete the sentences with the correct adverb of manner.

common _____	precise _____
efficient _____	rapid _rapidly_____
frequent _____	serious _____
immediate _____	successful _____

1. The temperature in New York can change very _rapidly_____. One day it's warm. The next day it's cold.

2. Doctors have not been able to _____ cure the common cold.

3. Modern cars use fuel more _____ than older cars do.

4. Hatem followed the instructions _____ because he didn't want to make a mistake.

5. Maria talks to her family _____. She calls them three or four times a week.

6. I need to think about the situation very _____ before I make a decision.

7. The doctor told Anita that her problem was serious. She needed to go to the hospital _____.

8. Orange trees are not _____ found in cold places.

TIP FOR SUCCESS

Don't overuse the adverbs *very* and *really*. They are useful general terms, but more specific adverbs give more information and make your writing more interesting.

B. CREATE Complete the sentences with your own ideas and opinions. Then read your sentences to a partner.

1. I think _____ is really interesting.

2. In my opinion _____ is extremely _____.

3. I can _____ fairly well.

4. For me _____ is extremely difficult.

5. I have had a(n) _____ _____ day today.

iQ PRACTICE Go online for more practice with adverbs of manner and degree.
Practice > Unit 8 > Activities 11–12

Write an explanatory paragraph about an illness

OBJECTIVE ▶

In this assignment, you will write an explanatory paragraph about an illness. You will include an explanation of the topic and information on how the illness can be prevented. As you prepare your paragraph, think about the Unit Question, "How can we prevent diseases?" Use information from Reading 1, Reading 2, the unit video, and your work in this unit to support your writing. Refer to the Self-Assessment checklist on page 194.

iQ PRACTICE   Go online to the Writing Tutor to read a model explanatory paragraph. *Practice > Unit 8 > Activity 13*

PLAN AND WRITE

A. BRAINSTORM Complete these activities.

1. Brainstorm a list for each question. Write down as many ideas as you can.

   • What illnesses do you know of that can spread from person to person?

   • What are some illnesses that you or someone you know have had?

   • What illnesses have you learned about recently?

2. Discuss your ideas with a partner.

3. Choose the illness you are going to write about.

TIP FOR SUCCESS

When you write an explanatory paragraph, keep your audience in mind. You should write about questions that the average person might have. Your explanations should be informative, but not too long. Be sure to include useful and interesting information that a reader may not know.

B. PLAN Organize the information about your topic. Remember, your goal is to provide useful information to your readers.

1. Complete these questions about the illness you chose. Then write notes to answer each question.

   a. What is _____?

   _____

   _____

   b. What are the symptoms of _____?

   _____

   _____

   c. How is _____ different from other diseases?

   _____

   _____

   d. Who gets _____?

   _____

   _____

e. How does _____ spread?

_____

_____

f. How can you avoid getting _____?

_____

_____

g. How can we prevent the spread of _____?

_____

_____

2. Look at your notes. Is there any information you will not include? Is there any additional information that you want to include? Make any changes needed.

3. What additional information do you need? Where can you get that information? Find the information you need and add it to your notes.

iQ RESOURCES Go online to download and complete the outline for your explanatory paragraph. *Resources > Writing Tools > Unit 8 > Outline*

C. WRITE Use your planning notes to write your paragraph.

1. Write your paragraph, using your notes in Activity B. Be sure that your explanatory paragraph clearly explains the illness. Try to use some adverbs of manner and degree.

2. Look at the Self-Assessment checklist on page 194 to guide your writing.

iQ PRACTICE Go online to the Writing Tutor to write your assignment. *Practice > Unit 8 > Activity 14*

REVISE AND EDIT

iQ RESOURCES Go online to download the peer review worksheet.
Resources > Writing Tools > Unit 8 > Peer Review Worksheet

A. PEER REVIEW Read your partner's paragraph. Then use the peer review worksheet. Discuss the review with your partner.

B. REWRITE Based on your partner's review, revise and rewrite your paragraph.

C. EDIT Complete the Self-Assessment checklist as you prepare to write the final draft of your explanatory paragraph. Be prepared to hand in your work or discuss it in class.

SELF-ASSESSMENT	Yes	No
Did you clearly define the illness with explanations and examples?	☐	☐
Do you have a good variety of adverbs of manner and degree? Did you use the correct word order?	☐	☐
Did you use collocations to make your writing sound more natural?	☐	☐
Does the explanatory paragraph include vocabulary from the unit?	☐	☐
Did you check your paragraph for punctuation, spelling, and grammar?	☐	☐

D. REFLECT Discuss these questions with a partner or group.

1. What is something new you learned in this unit?

2. Look back at the Unit Question—How can we prevent diseases? Is your answer different now than when you started the unit? If yes, how is it different? Why?

iQ PRACTICE Go to the online discussion board to discuss the questions.
Practice > Unit 8 > Activity 15

TRACK YOUR SUCCESS

iQ PRACTICE Go online to check the words and phrases you have learned in this unit. *Practice* › *Unit 8* › *Activity 16*

Check (✓) the skills and strategies you learned. If you need more work on a skill, refer to the page(s) in parentheses.

READING	☐ I can synthesize information. (p. 177)
CRITICAL THINKING	☐ I can summarize main ideas. (p. 183)
VOCABULARY	☐ I can use collocations. (p. 185)
WRITING	☐ I can write an explanatory paragraph. (p. 187)
GRAMMAR	☐ I can use adverbs of manner and degree. (p. 190)

OBJECTIVE ▶ ☐ I can gather information and ideas to write an explanatory paragraph about an illness.

VOCABULARY LIST and CEFR CORRELATION

🔑 The **Oxford 3000™** is a list of the 3,000 core words that every learner of English needs to know. The words have been chosen based on their frequency in the Oxford English Corpus and relevance to learners of English. Every word is aligned to the CEFR, guiding learners on the words they should know at A1-B2 level.

OPAL The **Oxford Phrasal Academic Lexicon** is an essential guide to the most important words and phrases to know for academic English. The word lists are based on the Oxford Corpus of Academic English and the British Academic Spoken English corpus.

The **Common European Framework of Reference for Language (CEFR)** provides a basic description of what language learners have to do to use language effectively. The system contains 6 reference levels: A1, A2, B1, B2, C1, C2.

UNIT 1

clear *(adj.)* 🔑 OPAL A2
connect *(v.)* 🔑 OPAL A2
contribute *(v.)* 🔑 OPAL B2
express *(v.)* 🔑 OPAL A2
find out *(v. phr.)* A1
influence *(v.)* 🔑 OPAL B1
psychologist *(n.)* 🔑 B2
purchase *(n.)* 🔑 B2
recommend *(v.)* 🔑 OPAL A2
researcher *(n.)* 🔑 OPAL A2
review *(n.)* 🔑 OPAL A2
social *(adj.)* 🔑 OPAL A2
spread *(v.)* 🔑 B1
study *(n.)* 🔑 OPAL A1
trend *(n.)* 🔑 OPAL B1

UNIT 2

advertising *(n.)* 🔑 A2
affect *(v.)* 🔑 OPAL A2
character *(n.)* 🔑 OPAL A2
consider *(v.)* 🔑 OPAL A2
culture *(n.)* 🔑 OPAL A1
dependable *(adj.)* C1
encourage *(v.)* 🔑 OPAL B1
environment *(n.)* 🔑 OPAL A2
establish *(v.)* 🔑 OPAL B2

notice *(v.)* 🔑 A2
psychology *(n.)* 🔑 B2
represent *(v.)* 🔑 OPAL B1
service *(n.)* 🔑 OPAL A2
unaware *(adj.)* B1
universal *(adj.)* 🔑 OPAL B2
variety *(n.)* 🔑 OPAL A2

UNIT 3

advice *(n.)* 🔑 A1
appropriately *(adv.)* 🔑 OPAL B2
avoid *(v.)* 🔑 OPAL A2
awkward *(adj.)* 🔑 B2
behavior *(n.)* 🔑 A2
custom *(n.)* B1
firmly *(adv.)* 🔑 B2
gesture *(n.)* B2
informal *(adj.)* 🔑 A2
interrupt *(v.)* 🔑 B2
make a good impression *(v. phr.)* B1
manners *(n.)* 🔑 A2
respect *(n.)* 🔑 OPAL B1
take part in *(v. phr.)* A2
traditional *(adj.)* 🔑 OPAL A2
typical *(adj.)* 🔑 OPAL A2

UNIT 4

advantage *(n.)* 🔑 OPAL A2
artificial *(adj.)* 🔑 B2
ban *(v.)* 🔑 B1
energy *(n.)* 🔑 OPAL A2
equipment *(n.)* 🔑 A2
examine *(v.)* 🔑 OPAL B1
invent *(v.)* 🔑 A2
performance *(n.)* 🔑 OPAL B1
reason *(n.)* 🔑 OPAL A1
replace *(v.)* 🔑 OPAL A2
situation *(n.)* 🔑 OPAL A1
specific *(adj.)* 🔑 OPAL A2
take care of *(v. phr.)* A2
technology *(n.)* 🔑 OPAL A2
under pressure *(prep. phr.)* B2
unfair *(adj.)* 🔑 B1

UNIT 5

challenge *(n.)* 🔑 OPAL B1
corporation *(n.)* B2
courage *(n.)* 🔑 B2
depend on *(v. phr.)* OPAL A2
design *(v.)* 🔑 OPAL A1
enthusiasm *(n.)* 🔑 B2
expand *(v.)* 🔑 OPAL B1
expert *(n.)* 🔑 OPAL A2

fail *(v.)* 🔑 OPAL **A2**
goal *(n.)* 🔑 OPAL **A2**
lifestyle *(n.)* 🔑 **A2**
manage *(v.)* 🔑 **A2**
pass down *(v. phr.)* **B2**
realistic *(adj.)* 🔑 **B2**
responsibility *(n.)* 🔑 OPAL **B1**
strength *(n.)* 🔑 OPAL **B1**
talent *(n.)* 🔑 **B1**
unity *(n.)* **B2**

UNIT 6

access *(v.)* 🔑 OPAL **B1**
assist *(v.)* 🔑 **B1**
automatically *(adv.)* **B2**
benefit *(v.)* OPAL **B1**
comfort zone *(n. phr.)* **C1**
concept *(n.)* 🔑 OPAL **B2**
decrease *(v.)* 🔑 OPAL **B2**
eventually *(adv.)* 🔑 **B1**
frustrated *(adj.)* **C1**
interact *(v.)* OPAL **B2**
internal *(adj.)* 🔑 OPAL **B2**
pace *(n.)* 🔑 **B2**
period *(n.)* 🔑 OPAL **A1**
physical *(n.)* 🔑 OPAL **A2**
process *(v.)* 🔑 OPAL **B2**
productive *(adj.)* OPAL **C1**
provide *(v.)* 🔑 OPAL **A2**
respond *(v.)* 🔑 OPAL **A2**
skip *(v.)* **C1**
unique *(adj.)* 🔑 OPAL **B2**

UNIT 7

a better understanding of *(n. phr.)* **B1**
ancient *(adj.)* 🔑 **A2**
as a result *(prep. phr.)* OPAL **A2**
attitude *(n.)* 🔑 OPAL **B1**
benefit from *(v. phr.)* **B1**
connected *(adj.)* **A2**
divide into *(v. phr.)* **B1**
emotional *(adj.)* 🔑 OPAL **B2**
experience *(n.)* 🔑 OPAL **A2**
found that *(v. phr.)* OPAL **A2**
generous *(adj.)* 🔑 **B1**
government *(n.)* 🔑 OPAL **A2**
plant *(v.)* 🔑 **A2**
relax *(v.)* 🔑 **A1**
remarkable *(adj.)* **B2**
surround *(v.)* 🔑 **B2**
unable *(adj.)* 🔑 **B1**
wildlife *(n.)* 🔑 **B2**

UNIT 8

contagious *(adj.)* **C1**
contaminated *(adj.)* **C1**
cover *(v.)* 🔑 **A2**
cure *(n.)* 🔑 **B2**
develop *(v.)* 🔑 OPAL **A2**
emergency *(n.)* 🔑 **B1**
extremely *(adv.)* 🔑 **A2**
fever *(n.)* **B2**
infect *(v.)* **C1**
outbreak *(n.)* **C1**
prevention *(n.)* 🔑 OPAL **C1**
related to *(adj. phr.)* OPAL **B1**
risk *(n.)* 🔑 OPAL **B1**
severe *(adj.)* 🔑 **B2**
source *(n.)* 🔑 OPAL **A2**
symptom *(n.)* 🔑 **B1**
take steps *(v. phr.)* **B1**
treat *(v.)* 🔑 OPAL **B1**
virus *(n.)* 🔑 **A2**
volunteer *(v.)* 🔑 **B1**

AUTHORS AND CONSULTANTS

AUTHORS

Joe McVeigh holds a B.A. in English and American Literature from Brown University and an M.A. in TESOL from Biola University. He teaches at Saint Michael's College and at Middlebury College and taught previously at universities in California. He has also lived and worked in a variety of countries. He regularly gives workshops and plenaries at ELT conferences around the world. He is a consultant, teacher-trainer, workshop presenter, and author; an English Language Specialist for the U.S. Department of State; and serves on the Board of Directors of the TESOL International Association.

Jennifer Bixby holds an M.A. in TESOL from Boston University. She has taught students of all ages in Colombia, Japan, and the United States in a wide variety of programs, including community colleges and intensive English programs. She has presented at numerous conferences on the topics of materials development and the teaching of reading and writing. She is a coauthor of the *Inside Writing* series published by Oxford University Press. Jennifer is an experienced ELT editor, writer, and author and has worked for many major publishers. Her specialties are materials for adult and university-bound students.

SERIES CONSULTANTS

Lawrence J. Zwier holds an M.A. in TESL from the University of Minnesota. He is currently the Associate Director for Curriculum Development at the English Language Center at Michigan State University in East Lansing. He has taught ESL/EFL in the United States, Saudi Arabia, Malaysia, Japan, and Singapore.

Marguerite Ann Snow holds a Ph.D. in Applied Linguistics from UCLA. She teaches in the TESOL M.A. program in the Charter College of Education at California State University, Los Angeles. She was a Fulbright scholar in Hong Kong and Cyprus. In 2006, she received the President's Distinguished Professor award at CSULA. She has trained ESL teachers in the United States and EFL teachers in more than 25 countries. She is the author/editor of numerous publications in the areas of content-based instruction, English for academic purposes, and standards for English teaching and learning. She is a co-editor of *Teaching English as a Second or Foreign Language* (4th ed.).

CRITICAL THINKING CONSULTANT James Dunn is a Junior Associate Professor at Tokai University and the Coordinator of the JALT Critical Thinking Special Interest Group. His research interests include critical thinking skills' impact on student brain function during English learning as measured by EEG. His educational goals are to help students understand that they are capable of more than they might think and to expand their cultural competence with critical thinking and higher-order thinking skills.

ASSESSMENT CONSULTANT Elaine Boyd has worked in assessment for over 30 years for international testing organizations. She has designed and delivered courses in assessment literacy and is also the author of several EL exam coursebooks for leading publishers. She is an Associate Tutor (M.A. TESOL/Linguistics) at University College, London. Her research interests are classroom assessment, issues in managing feedback, and intercultural competences.

VOCABULARY CONSULTANT Cheryl Boyd Zimmerman is Professor Emeritus at California State University, Fullerton. She specialized in second-language vocabulary acquisition, an area in which she is widely published. She taught graduate courses on second-language acquisition, culture, vocabulary, and the fundamentals of TESOL, and has been a frequent invited speaker on topics related to vocabulary teaching and learning. She is the author of *Word Knowledge: A Vocabulary Teacher's Handbook* and Series Director of *Inside Reading, Inside Writing*, and *Inside Listening and Speaking*, published by Oxford University Press.

ONLINE INTEGRATION Chantal Hemmi holds an Ed.D. TEFL and is a Japan-based teacher trainer and curriculum designer. Since leaving her position as Academic Director of the British Council in Tokyo, she has been teaching at the Center for Language Education and Research at Sophia University in an EAP/CLIL program offered for undergraduates. She delivers lectures and teacher trainings throughout Japan, Indonesia, and Malaysia.

COMMUNICATIVE GRAMMAR CONSULTANT Nancy Schoenfeld holds an M.A. in TESOL from Biola University in La Mirada, California, and has been an English language instructor since 2000. She has taught ESL in California and Hawaii and EFL in Thailand and Kuwait. She has also trained teachers in the United States and Indonesia. Her interests include teaching vocabulary, extensive reading, and student motivation. She is currently an English Language Instructor at Kuwait University.